From Stilettos to Grace
Tiffany Brearton

SQUARE TREE PUBLISHING
www.SquareTreePublishing.com

For more information about bulk purchases, please contact
Square Tree Publishing at info@squaretreepublishing.com.

Cover design by Sharon Marta

Photography for Cover Design: Allison Darling
Website : www.allisondarlingphotography.com

ISBN 978-1-957293-06-6

Table of Contents

Dedication

First, I want to thank God, for without Him, my mess is just a mess. He carried me through when I could not take one more step. He has redeemed my story and given me hope for my future.

Acknowledgements

Thank you to my husband Dustin, who has supported me through so much of this journey. I know it hasn't always been easy, but you do it anyway, and I am so thankful. You get up every morning to go out and provide for us. You are consistent in your love and support. You are the man of my dreams, and I love you so much. You balance me in ways I didn't know I even needed to be balanced. Thank you for always being the solid rock for our family. Marrying you, my love, is the best decision I ever made!

Thank you to my children, McKenzie, Lincoln, Charity, and Jasmine. You are the greatest God-given blessings of my life. You have taught me to love and live in ways I never thought possible. I don't know what I did to deserve to be blessed with all of you, but I am overwhelmed with gratitude for each of you. Always remember how loved and how amazing you are. Anything is possible with God, and I hope someday you see that in Mom's journey, too.

Thank you to my mom and dad. You both have been to hell and back with me and have always been there to help when I needed it. I know it has not been an easy ride, but thank you for always standing by me. I love you.

Thank you to my friends. There are way too many of you to name, but each of you have played a more significant role in my life than you could ever have imagined. You have allowed me to grow into my God-given identity and loved me through the process. You embraced my "too much" and didn't allow any of the darkness to scare you away. I am forever grateful for the safe place each of you has given me. I love you.

Thank you to my church and church family. Thank you for allowing and facilitating groups that so many other churches shy away from. Thank you for providing spaces for me to discover that I was not crazy but instead experiencing very normal side effects of trauma, and for showing me that healing was possible for my brain. My hope is that my journey and your model will show other churches that these topics should be addressed, and healing is possible for all of God's children.

Endorsements
Tiffany Brearton, *From Stilettos to Grace*

"Every life carries a message of God's grace. Perhaps, a broken life makes that message even greater. You will marvel at the grace of God that flows through each chapter of this book. Tiffany Brearton has pulled back layer after layer of her heart to show you how good God truly is. Your soul will be moved as you read how Tiffany has overcome great darkness and pain to become a great light of joy and victory in today's world. *From Stilettos to Grace* is going to change your life and nudge you closer to the heart of God!"

—Dr. Brian Simmons
Passion & Fire Ministries,
Lead translator of the **Passion Translation Bible**

"Blessed are those that overcome! This is a statement repeated throughout Scripture. Jesus attached promises for those that overcome and even says that those who have been forgiven much, love much. Tiffany gives God the glory in testifying of His faithfulness to take her *From Stilettos to Grace.* May you experience God's goodness as you read this amazing book."

—Richie Seltzer,
Evangelist with **Global Awakening**

"If you have ever wondered how far God's arm will reach to redeem His children, then this book is for you. Testimonies are a powerful way to stir up the imagination and present 'God possibilities.' Tiffany does an excellent job doing just this, by telling her story of redemption in Christ. It is big, and it is bold. However, the way she writes ensures that the reader knows God is the Author of her story; that He is the One who ordained all her days This is an excellent read that stirs up our imaginations in Christ and reminds us of His unconditional love and power. You won't be disappointed."

—Lisa Schwarz,
Founder and **CEO of Crazy8 Ministries** and author of
Enforcing You

"Many people are losing hope in humanity and the future generations. Tiffany has so bravely told her story of the tragic levels of trauma that destroyed her view of herself. She would, in most ways, represent someone that the world would see as too far gone. But when Jesus walks into her story, the impossible becomes the inevitable. Healing!"

—Todd Pierce,
Riding High Ministries, Inc.

"*From Stilettos to Grace* is a dynamic glimpse of a woman's journey facing multiple traumas that impacted her life from childhood to adulthood through the deep pursuit of inner healing after years of traumatic experiences. Throughout this book, Tiffany shares her life with such vivid transparency that you feel as if you are with her along the journey. She shares the heartache of feeling unseen, experiencing traumatic and abusive relationships, and grief due to several losses, but also her persistent determination to see her dreams fulfilled in her life. Tiffany's story will resonate with women who feel unworthy, unloved, discarded, or unvalued due to past traumas. This book will reveal an important revelation to women: What happened to you *matters* and nothing is wrong with you; your story matters! Tiffany's words cut through lies like stilettos on a hard floor. Her story provides hope to readers that no matter the darkness, despair, sadness, or how gloomy it seems, there is still hope. Tiffany's authentic re-telling of her journey through abusive relationships and the loss of a spouse was heartfelt and touching. In her hardest moments, Tiffany's heart was drawn back to the Lord as she realized His deep love for her.

This memoir is a brave and powerful mustread by a woman who has lost so much and has received much restoration. I believe this book will be a beacon of hope for many women who are in search of hope, healing, and new beginnings."

—Dr. Amanda Helman
Author, Breakthrough Coach, Speaker
Founder of **Healthy Roots LLC**

"*From Stilettos to Grace* is a book needed for our time. It takes readers through Tiffany's journey experiencing sexual abuse, the loss of a husband to cancer, and a magnificent climax of God's healing. Tiffany takes an unflinching and vulnerable look at her life as a stripper and abuse survivor to show how God can truly work miracles if you simply open up to Him. If you love stories of triumph, you will love this book."

—Jennifer Osborn,
author of *A Beautiful Healing*

"Anyone who has ever felt scared or helpless should read this book. Tiffany is passionate and determined to overcome the demons in her life that have tried to hold her back. This is a spirit-lead woman who I have had the privilege of witnessing pursue freedom, redemption, and healing. I've had a front row seat to her chasing after answers, not only for herself, but for others as well. Tiffany continues to widen that path of freedom for those around her who have gone through similar circumstances. Tiffany's heartbreaking, gut-wrenching journey to healing is a story that we all need and can relate to."

—Jenny Becknell

"When I first met Tiffany, she shared her incredible testimony of transformation with me. She was one of the first guests on my show, *Voices of Recovery*. It takes courage to share our stories with the world. Like other guests, Tiffany desires to point people to Jesus, the One who sets the captives free. What people need to see are authentic survivors of trauma and abuse who are willing to testify about their scars so people understand what caused the wound and Who initiated the miraculous healing. Since I have known her, I have watched Tiffany emerge out of her chrysalis into the beautiful and unique butterfly that God destined her to become. Now it's time for her to fly!"

—Michele Eich, author of
How to Kill an Addiction: Recovery with God
Voices of Recovery

"Tiffany's raw and transparent retelling of her own story of sexual trauma is eye opening. Through her authentic sharing, she exposes the frequency of sexual abuse, rape, and emotional trauma. As a pastor, my hope is that Tiffany's vulnerability will help those in the church who have any history of sexual abuse feel the freedom to discuss it among those they worship with regularly. Her desire is that people are set free and find healing in the life that only Christ can give."

—Andre Rusch, Lead Pastor,
The Church at Clayton Crossings

"Tiffany Brearton's extraordinary story is like no other. Her demonstration of faith, trust, and obedience is a testimony of how God uses even the worst of situations and brokenness to restore and to create a renewed life. Upon completing the last page of her book, I felt the Lord remind me of the song *Diamonds* by Hawk Nelson. Tiffany's story of redemption— as an overcomer—is not only a miracle in itself, but also a testimony that shines light into the darkness that brings a message of hope and freedom to all. Tiffany is no longer a 'diamond in the rough' but a polished gem that shines as a beautiful woman of God."

—Brad Fahrenkamp, Fahrenkamp Ministries

"Tiffany's story tells of the redeeming hope that is available to all. No one is outside the reach of God's grace, forgiveness, and love. Her story is an encouraging reminder that when we can't make sense of what is happening in life, and can't see how circumstances could possibly turn around, the Creator is watching over us and knows how to draw us near."

—Dana Schmoyer, YouTuber
Reclaiming Motherhood

Introduction

Yesterday was hard, but it's gone, and I am still here. This
space I am in right now is glorious compared to where I
have been. The cost was high, but the reward was HUGE!
It is not measurable and often I do not understand it, but it
is priceless. Worth more than any diamond or ruby on the
planet and to sit in it today—it was worth it all.

The wholeness journey, the chase for healing, the
desire of my heart, all to achieve one verse in the Bible.
The constant pursuit, the never giving up, the therapy, the
vulnerability, the prayers, the surrender, the forgiveness, and
the deliverance all to hear…

*"And He said to her, 'Daughter, your faith has made
you well, go in peace.'" (Luke 8:48 ESV)*

I needed that peace. I was desperate for it. I tasted
it like it was a drug I couldn't live without. It tasted whole,
it tasted complete, it tasted FREE. It was so hard; it was so
real. To get here I had to put everything out there and hold
nothing back. I had to sit in the dark alone many times. I
had to hurt people I loved so deeply. I had to forgive those
who have hurt me, and even more difficult, I had to forgive
myself. I had to be brave, I had to be okay with looking like
a fool on more than one occasion. I had to let go of control
and surrender it all to *Him.* So, I chased Him with everything

I had. I brought others in on the chase with me. I ran hard and I didn't give up until finally, *finally*…I found the release that I had been chasing.

This beautiful journey has been gloomy at times but nothing short of a miracle. But to truly see the miracle, I have to take you back to where it all began. Miracles only happen when there is a need for them. My need had been brewing for quite some time.

Chapter 1
Beginnings

I was born In Northern Kentucky on June 3, 1981, to Dennis and Darlene. I was the middle child of three, sandwiched between by sister, who is three years older, and my brother, who is two years younger than me. I grew up across the street from our family farm, then moved into the farm when I was in middle school. My father had an incredible work ethic and always thrived in business. He also had a strong passion to continue in his father's footsteps and take care of the family farm. He often worked all day long at the office and then on the farm until well after dark, only to get up and do it again the next day. My mother stayed home and cared for us when we were young and then went back to work as we grew and went to school. Before us kids came around, she did pretty well in the real estate business and decided to pursue that field again for a while before moving on to some other jobs.

I grew up in a normal home environment, for the most part. There was, of course, some heartache along the way, but I suspect it is that way in every family. My dad was the outdoor type, and I was not, so he naturally seemed to connect more with my younger brother, who loved the outdoors as well. As early as I can remember, I was in constant competition with my younger brother. I'm not sure he was even aware of the competition or "playing the game," but I sure was. I desperately wanted to be seen the way he was, so much so that I forgot who I was, somewhere in there. I tried to fit in a box I was never intended to be in. I became the constant pleaser. I was always trying to prove something—that I was better to others, but even more trying to prove it to myself. Somewhere along the way, I told my little girl self I was not enough, and this mindset dictated my actions, thoughts, and feelings every single day. The pursuit of "good enough" and acceptance started before I can even remember.

As a child, I entertained who paid attention to me. I fed off the attention like a baby feeds off milk. Attention and acceptance were my drug of choice then, and I did anything to get it. If you wanted to have a fun party, I was on your invite list. I was constantly making up dance routines and comedy acts to perform for anyone who would watch. I dreamed of having my name in lights one day. If you didn't like me, I did everything I could to change your mind. I was constantly "on." I had to be the center of attention; I was starving for it, and winning someone's attention meant I was winning my own made-up game.

My older sister was a lot more quiet than I was. She always seemed so mature and grown up. We always had a good relationship, but I am not sure how well we related to each other as kids. I had a big, outgoing personality and she was an introvert. When I came along, I am sure that must have disrupted the peace she enjoyed, but I don't remember her ever saying that. My younger brother, on the other hand, was a lot more like me. We played well together (most of the time) but we also fought like cats and dogs. Like I said, it felt like we were always in constant competition. He was not quiet either. My brother was a bit mischievous for sure, and often found himself in trouble. My parents found it a little difficult to control him. For the most part though, he was the one who played with me.

My Parents

My mom was my rescuer. It didn't matter what kind of trouble I got into; she always stuck up for me. She had a very loving heart and saw something special in me that others could not see. My mom was an emotional "feeler" like me and understood me better. My dad was more the disciplinarian. He liked order in his household and wanted to make sure everything was in tip-top shape. As I mentioned, he was a very hard worker and always made sure his family was provided for. Looking back now, they really were a good combination together. They did a really good job playing the good cop/bad cop roles, and although I am sure he didn't always like to be the bad guy, he always wanted what was best for us.

My parents gave us so many unique and fun experiences growing up. For a while, we had a few foreign exchange students live with us, and we traveled at least once a year. Once, my parents somehow arranged for me to be the bat girl for the Cincinnati Reds. Wow, was that exciting!

At the time, my little girl self had a crush on Paul O'Neil, and that day I had the opportunity to meet him *and* get my picture taken with him for the newspaper!

I really do admire my parents for doing the best they could do with a child like me. I wouldn't have said that back then while growing up. Sometimes you just need some distance from the situation to really see the effects. Tiffany as a child was starved for attention, and no matter how much attention and love she received, it was NEVER enough. I carried this with me well into adulthood. It was like to trying to fill a bottomless pit. I am thankful to have had parents who, while they may not have been perfect, never gave up on me and were there for me no matter what.

Dramatic Shift

In middle school something shifted—that carefree and trusting attitude. A favorite cousin of mine came to live with us. My dad was very firm in his parenting and had high hopes that he could change the young boy's life around. He was just a teenager but had been in and out of trouble most of his life. The news of him coming to live with us was welcomed from me. I was so excited to be able to spend more time with him.

He was five or so years older than me, and I thought he was super cool. We became really close during his time living with us. Honestly, he just started to feel like an older brother to me. I became very comfortable around him and would climb all over him like a jungle gym. I was a very affectionate child, seeking attention, as you already know.

One winter morning the snow had begun to fall, and we all gathered around the television cuddled up together. We watched the news and waited with great anticipation as the school closings flashed across the screen. When we had first turned the television on, we had just missed the schools beginning with the letter C. We were looking for Campbell County, so we had to wait until it came all the way back around to find out that we were indeed closed. We decided to go back to bed and get some rest, and I cuddled up in bed with my cousin and went to sleep.

Shortly after drifting off, I was awakened by his hands on my body. I was very confused as my cousin started to rock his body against mine and began touching me underneath my underwear. I was a very immature built 7th grader, nowhere near the age of puberty, and had no clue what he was doing other than knowing it did not feel right and I wanted it to stop. I am still not sure what happened after that or how far things went. It was as if I had blacked out and no longer was in my body. At some point, I pretended to sleepwalk into my mom's room and hop in bed next to her. As I lay under the covers in her bed, I was so scared I didn't utter a word. My brain was trying to process what had just happened, but my sweet, innocent little girl self had no clue what had occurred. Terrified and trembling, I laid next to my mom. She had no clue what had just happened to her baby girl just a couple rooms away. I wish I could have told her then but honestly, that sweet little girl didn't have the language for what had just occurred.

As time went on, I was desperate for him to move out of our house. He went from my best bud to my worst enemy. It was like living in hell and being tormented and tortured in my own home. Suddenly, my safe place became a nightmare. He constantly teased and stalked me, walking behind me everywhere I went, and I had no place to go. I was terrified. That once trusting little girl was gone.

Chapter 2
Damage Done

The end of that school year came, and on my birthday, June 3, my parents unknowingly gave me the best birthday present they had ever given me: They dropped my cousin off, back with his mother, for good. At last, he was out of my face!

Unfortunately, his absence did not automatically stop the torture like I thought it would. The damage was already done, and my need for attention shifted to a desperate cry for help. I was dying inside from the pain.

My Grandparents

Another hard blow happened in those middle school years. My very best friend, my grandpa, was diagnosed with cancer and died shortly after. My grandpa was my world, and I was his world—at least he made me feel like I was, anyway. He was the best storyteller. I would sit around and hang onto every word that came out of his mouth, believing everything he said as the absolute truth. Once, he pointed up to a plane in the sky and told us that that plane was the one he'd flown during the war. My brother and sister laughed, but I didn't; in fact, I was mad at them for laughing at my grandpa. He could do no wrong in my eyes. We often sat outside on milk crates, talking and enjoying each other's company. In the summertime, he would grab the very first watermelon from the garden, pull out his pocketknife, and cut it up so we could enjoy that sweet, juicy watermelon outside together. He was my favorite person in the whole world and my hero.

I was super close to my grandma and grandpa also because they had always lived nearby. When I was in elementary school and both my parents were working, I often went to the office and told them I was sick so my grandparents would pick me up. We'd spend the whole day together. Let's just say I spent most of the second grade playing a lot of hooky.

When my family moved to the farm, less than a mile from my grandparents' house, we became even closer. Every Monday after school, I spent a few hours with them at their house. It was my night! My grandmother would make her famous vegetable soup for me, along with brownies for dessert. As soon as I walked in the door, I could smell those delicious brownies. What I would do to be back in that room with them enjoying those moments! A few hours with them was never enough. Most every Monday evening I would talk my grandpa into calling my parents and asking if I could spend the night. They said no almost every time, and I would walk home, sad and in tears.

Spiraling Out of Control

When my grandfather died, my life seemed to spiral out of control. The pain was so unbearable at times that I found myself cutting my arms with a box cutter, looking for some measure of relief from the emotional pain. It became something I did almost every day after school. I kept the little box cutter in my desk drawer and ran it across my arms when I got home. The more I hid my pain, the worse I felt. I didn't know what was happening, but my mental health was severely impacted. I was never big or overweight—in fact, I was always smaller than kids my age—but suddenly I began to see myself differently. Honestly, I am not sure how I came up with this idea on my own (maybe I saw it on TV?), but I began to starve myself. When I wasn't doing that, I would eat, but then I would throw up my food or take laxatives. I began to leave suicide notes out all the time, hoping someone would find them and save me.

I was dying on the inside, so a physical death would surely stop the pain. I had come up with a plan for how I was going to do it. I was going to wait until everyone went to sleep, and then I was going to sneak out of bed and drink the chemicals under the bathroom sink. But when I learned that if you killed yourself you couldn't go to heaven, I couldn't go through with it. I couldn't imagine the thought of never seeing my grandfather again someday. I don't know who taught me that, but that little line, true or not, kept me alive.

My parents did the best they could. I am not sure anyone truly knows how to properly handle a troubled child, especially when they didn't know what was really going on. However, they did know they had to do *something*, because they had a daughter crying out that she was going to kill herself almost every day. They tried to help me by sending me to a couple different counselors and putting me on medication. The medication was terrible, and I couldn't continue taking it. I went from lots of emotions to no emotions at all with those pills, and I knew that wasn't good for me either. The counselors really didn't work because, again, they didn't really know what was behind it all. I told them I had suicidal thoughts, but they never found out why. I don't believe I ever thought about telling them about the sexual abuse; I just knew I needed help. What I didn't know at the time was that my help would come from dealing with that issue.

Next Steps

I made it through my teenage years—just barely—and the minute I turned eighteen, I moved out of the house. I didn't move too far, just up the hill to my grandmother's house. My grandma was relaxed and open minded. There weren't many rules to follow, which is why it seemed so appealing. My friends all thought my grandma was the coolest. I used to drive her to Walmart so she could do her shopping, and then we'd eat in the little food court, and she would buy me cigarettes as payment. I would smoke in the car while driving her. She even kept an ashtray so I could smoke inside her house.

A few weeks after I graduated, my friends had made plans for the future, and I still didn't know what my next step was. I knew I wanted to be an actress. In fact, I had dreamt about it for as long as I could remember but didn't have a clue how to make it happen. I knew most actors lived in New York City, so I decided to start saving money so I could go to college at NYU. While I hadn't sorted out the logistics yet, I knew I needed a lot of money fast if I wanted to make it happen in the near future. I quickly brainstormed and somehow came to the conclusion that I was going to be a stripper. I grabbed a phone book and looked up addresses of the closest strip clubs. I found some nearby in Newport, Kentucky, and headed there.

I must have blacked out or something because most of the details of that moment left me. I couldn't even begin to tell you where I parked or what the place looked like. I do, however, remember one thing: an older man sitting at the bar named Marvin. Marvin told me that I was too young to work there and wouldn't be able to dance there until I was twenty. He told me about another strip club in Lawrenceburg, Indiana, that hired eighteen-year-old girls and gave me directions. So, off I went. I am not even sure how I had the courage at such a young age to walk into a strip club. I wasn't just a young, naïve eighteen-year-old girl, but I was also still a virgin and had no real concept of what I was about to walk into.

The Job

I arrived at the club in Indiana and let the doorman know I was looking for a job. I was escorted back to the back office area for an interview. On the way in, we walked past the lap dance area. This moment in time really sticks out to me because it was the first time in my life I had ever seen anything like that. I remember fearfully asking the manager if I would have to do those. He, of course, answered, "Yes."

I am sure he got a real kick out of that question later. I mean, really? What was I thinking, walking into a strip club for a job wondering if I was going to have to give a lap dance? I clearly didn't know what to think at the time.

I was quickly hired, and they roped me into the day shift position. The manager gave me a quick tour and introduced me to some of the girls. One of the girls who came up to meet me was completely topless and acting like it was absolutely normal. I had never in my life before had a conversation with another woman who was almost completely naked. But here I was, trying to pretend like I was completely comfortable in this situation.

Playing the Part

They gave me some suggestions for costumes to buy, just to get me started, and off I went. I had very little money, so I ended up at Walmart trying to piece together an outfit for as cheap as possible. I grabbed a couple of tube tops for my first stripper costume. One would function as a mini skirt and the other as my top.

I started the next day more scared than I've ever been. All of the girls shared a dressing room, and I was so nervous to get undressed in there in front of everyone, how was I going to get undressed on stage? Luckily, day shift was typically slow, so I could ease my way into it. Each girl would dance two songs on stage and then rotate back around after all the other girls had gone. The first song I was to dance in my costume, but during the second song I had to strip down to just my thong.

I was shaking from head to toe as I lifted my foot to walk up on that stage. The first song played, and it was all a blur. I wish I could remember the songs I picked, but the trauma from this event erased it from my head, I suppose. As the second song began, I headed toward the back of the stage to prepare for the "strip down." In that moment, I had never felt so physically exposed. I am sure the other girls' strip downs were far more sexy than mine—, but honestly, I didn't even know what sexy was at this time. I was still just a little girl who had never had sex. There I was in a room full of strangers in the most vulnerable, intimate position, with nothing on but my underwear. Everyone looked on to check out the new girl's "goods." This often happened as a way to check out the competition. Sadly, it didn't really seem to matter what the girl's face looked like or how nice she was. It was always the moment during the second song as the dancer removed her clothes that all eyes were on her. It was a competitive environment in that way. I was immediately seen as competition, and others even seemed to question my honesty about my body being real.

As the hours went on, men began to arrive, it was time for me to finally work up the courage to go talk to them. I was trembling but pushed past the fear as I walked up and sat down next to one of the male customers. I wasn't there to take off my clothes for free, so I had to push past the fear. He found out that it was my first day and that I had never given a lap dance before. He was ready to change that and be my first, but I was not sure *I* was ready. I stuffed my own feelings about it deep down inside, and off we went.

As the song began, I stayed as far away from him as possible. It wasn't much of a "lap" dance. Every time I got close to him, he would thrust his pelvis into the air, and I would quickly retreat back again. It may have been the worst lap dance of all time, but looking back now, I wish I had done every lap dance this way. I think he wanted to see if he could take advantage of the new girl, but thankfully I stood my ground. He only purchased one dance and was quite the regular, but he never got another lap dance from me again.

Chapter 3
Striptease and Red Flags

As I settled into being a stripper, I began to relax and become more confident—or rather, I suppressed my feelings enough that I became numb to the environment, which made it more tolerable.

When I realized I wasn't making enough money on day shift, I began working the night shift. At some point I decided if I was going to take off my clothes, I was going to have to make a lot of money doing it. The only way a guy in that club was going to get to spend time with me was in the lap dance area, where I got paid $15 a song. If I walked up to you, it was to ask one question: "Do you want a lap dance?" If the answer was no, then away I went to the next guy. For me, sitting down with a guy over a drink was too personal. It was like dating, and they could get to know the real you. While I was dancing, I was an actress. I even had a stage name and was comfortable with playing the character. Talking, on the other hand, resulted in real life questions like, "How old are you? Where are you from?" and so on. At that point, they were getting to know the real me, and that was way too intimate for me.

At one point, I set a lap dance record of 52 lap dances in one shift. When I did a lap dance, I made sure to sit as close as humanly possible to the DJ/bouncer. His job was to announce the dancers on the stage and to oversee the lap dance area to make sure the dancers and customers were staying within the rules.

Sitting next to the DJ gave me a sense of safety. I began to make the DJ my best friend. I tipped him well and was always on my A game around him. I thought if I took care of him, he would take care of me. At my club, the DJ's name was Tim. Tim was a thirty-four-year-old man, and although short and stocky, he could take someone down if they got out of line. In fact, I had seen him do it quite a few times, which is what built more confidence in me. He once took this really big guy down right in front of me, and knowing he was capable of doing this made me feel so much safer.

I even began to make friends with a couple of the girls. That girl who first walked up to talk to me without her top on became one of my friends, and a couple other girls as well. I started to feel comfortable and let some boundaries down. Initially, I did not want to be friends with any of the dancers because, let's be honest, I was a virgin and I was trying to stay as pure as possible, but these girls were kind to me, and I began to trust them. They were all older than I was and sort of mothered me. Once they found out I was only eighteen and a virgin, either they wanted to take care of me or change that pure part of me. One evening, I agreed to go out dancing with them. On the way, we stopped at the local drug dealer's house, and they got some ecstasy. I was a nervous wreck and really didn't know what I had gotten myself into. This friend reassured me everything was going to be okay, so I continued with the evening. As the night went on, they convinced me to take half of a pill, and I eventually agreed. I had never taken any drugs except for trying marijuana a few times, so this was a whole new experience for me. We did have fun that evening, dancing the night away, but things got really trippy afterward. We ended up at some guy's house, and I had no idea who he was. The girls even tried to convince me to lose my virginity while on ecstasy. I really was not of sound mind but somehow was with it enough to say no.

The next day at work, still overcoming some of the effects of the drug, I made a silent pledge that I would never put myself in that position again, and that was the first and last time I hung out with that group of girls. Honestly, it was my fault for getting myself into that position, but knowing myself, I knew it was not a place where I could stand my ground.

I became closer to Tim because I found some sense of safety with him. During the day shift, we had a lot of extra time on our hands and could chat and get to know one another. Remember, I was just an eighteen-year-old girl, so talking to a thirty-four-year-old man made me feel special. We were developing what I thought to be a great friendship. One day, he asked me if I would like to go out to a club named Bourbon Street. A couple other girls were going, so I thought it was harmless. I loved to dance, so going to an adult club seemed super cool. When the evening began, everything seemed normal, but I soon realized Tim thought we were on a date. I was so confused and didn't want to lose my safety net at work, so I went along with it. I had spent my whole life trying to please others, so this was no different. I even tried to convince myself this relationship could be real and amazing. I was an eighteen-year-old virgin and he was a thirty-four year old man who worked in a strip club for years. Age is just a number, right?

Red Flags

The next time we worked together it seemed like we had become a thing. I don't even really know how it happened but again, I was a pleaser, so I went right along with it. Pretty soon it became easy to go along with. I was now the most protected girl in the place and I, for sure, liked that benefit. Tim's best friend was the manager there, too, so when Tim wasn't working Bill was and kept an eye on me as well.

Tim quickly started to tell me more about himself. One night, he revealed he was a dad of two twin boys who were thirteen years old, and this news raised some red flags. He showed me an adorable picture of the boys that he kept in his wallet. This picture was from when they were much younger. Learning that Tim was a father was too much for me. I mean, these little guys were closer to my age than their dad was! I was not sure I could step into a mother role with kids only five years younger than I was. This was my first adult relationship though, and I thought it was going to be a fairytale. So, being the awesome, people pleasing princess I was, I quickly convinced myself we could get through anything together as long as we were in love.

As our relationship progressed, I decided to share my big news of being a virgin with him. I had told a couple of the other dancers but was having a hard time telling Tim. I worked up the courage one night at work. He had come in to "visit" on his day off. He had some beers and bought some stacks of singles at the bar to throw all over me while I was onstage. He was feeling good by the end of the night, so as we were saying our goodbyes, I told him. I said, "I am a virgin, and I plan on staying that way until I know I love someone and know I am going to spend the rest of my life with them." Well, not long after I said that he told me he loved me and wanted to spend the rest of his life with me. I was on Cinderella's Cloud Nine! Finally, my Prince Charming had come and was going to rescue me from everything. All my walls began to fall down. He was "my person" and my "one true love," and I could trust him with everything. He would never hurt me. He was my knight in shining armor that I had always wished for, and my life was now going to be so much easier. Or so I thought. Do you think, maybe, I put too much hope into fairytales growing up? I really believed this was how relationships were supposed to be.

No Prince Charming

It came time for me to visit Tim's place. I thought he was rich because of all the money he threw all over me;

35

I'm talking, fifty to a hundred dollars every time I went up onstage. I thought his house was going to be something special. I walked into an apartment with hardly any furniture in it. His tiny television sat on a cardboard box. Red flags yet, again, I ignored. It wasn't about the money; it was about him and how safe he made me feel. I stuffed those feelings down deep and told myself the place was great.

One day, we began kissing on his bed and I somehow ended up with just my underwear on. I felt completely safe because that is the way he typically saw me. We had made out plenty of times before, but unfortunately, this time he would not stop. I told him no and was crying because of the pain I was in. He looked down at me with those dark eyes of his, saw the tears in my eyes, and told me not to worry— "The water works would start soon." I had no idea what he was talking about. I cried the whole time but he didn't care. The person I depended on for safety was now violating everything I thought was real. Whenever that dreadful act ended, I laid there crying and immediately felt dirty. Was this really what I had saved my virginity for? Suddenly, I felt so alone. He wasn't concerned that I was laying there next to him in tears. I think he fell asleep while I was crying.

I laid there shaking under the blanket, crying as I tried to process what had just happened. Didn't he love me? I had saved such a precious gift for my future husband and the words of wisdom he shared with me were, "Don't worry, the waterworks will start soon." I needed the pain to stop immediately, so I began to tell that little girl a story. "Oh, Tiffany…he loves you. He probably didn't hear you crying and yelling out, 'No!' He looked down at you and saw your tears and must have thought they were tears of joy."

So, I stayed, and I made it okay. I needed to fulfill the promise I had made to myself long ago, that the first person I had sex with I was going to marry. I was all in, and I stayed. He began to teach me about sex, and everything I thought sex was went out the window. He would dig his claws into my skin until I bled. I now thought this is what sex and love were supposed to be like. When I went to work, his claw marks were all over me. It was almost like his way of marking me. Others would see the marks on my body, and he bragged about it.

One day, as I got undressed and tried to figure out a way to cover the scratch marks on my skin, another sweet dancer stepped in to try to help me out. She was open about her desire to go to Vegas to become a prostitute, and she probably knew about the world of sex a little more than I did. I removed the rest of my clothing and let out a squeal from the pain of the air hitting my skin. She looked at me with deep concern in her eyes. She knew that just a few weeks ago I was a virgin, and now I was covered in wounds. She didn't say anything, but her eyes spoke to me, almost as if to say, "This is not right." She was concerned for my wellbeing and did not believe this is how I should be treated. She covered up the wounds and bruises the best she could with makeup, and we went on our way with work. The makeup in those wounds burned so bad, and the burning intensified as I worked up a sweat from dancing.

I was young and beautiful and was often questioned whether my body was real because of the perfect shape it was in. I was dating a not-so-perfect, overweight, angry older man, and I found myself chasing him for attention. There was another girl in the club who he had his eye on. She had come into some drug problems and would often pass out on men's laps during lap dances, and while she was unconscious, they could get away with a thing or two. I think Tim wanted to be her hero. He cared and was very loving toward her. I fantasized about him treating me that way. I watched his eyes follow her constantly as she walked across the bar in a daze. He deeply desired for something to be there, and she often played into it. Occasionally, he lent her money when she was in trouble with bills or drugs. I began to fall into that competitive cycle I had felt trapped in my whole life. Here I was in the best shape of my life, and after taking the gift of my virginity, I still wasn't good enough. So, the competition was on to show him I was worthy of his love and attention, and I was back in that vicious cycle of chasing others for the attention I so desperately craved.

Chapter 4
Warrants and a Wedding

Tim was really into sports memorabilia, so I took an interest also in my quest to become the perfect and only woman for him and the only one he desired. I began going to the sports card shop every single day after work, often leaving with boxes of baseball cards. This sounds harmless, but I spent at least $200 every time I walked into the store.

Occasionally, Tim spent his days off at a strip club in Louisville, where he spent all his money on one particular girl at the club. I decided to go with him, because surely this would make him like me more. When we got to the club, I was totally surprised because the girl he had his eyes on looked nothing like me. She was very tiny and small chested, whereas I had an hourglass figure and was large chested. I struggled to process why he pursued me in the first place. I looked completely different than the other two women he was interested in. I was young and beautiful, *and* I made the most money in the club I worked in. Why was I chasing this man's attention? This was the vicious cycle of competition I was in.

I was determined to make him want me, believing our love was worth fighting for at all costs. So, that was exactly what I was going to do. I was going to handle my fear of losing him by doing whatever it took to make myself more appealing for him, even if that meant not being myself at all.

Tim found seeing girls kissing attractive and he gave me permission to invite some girls over. I invited two girls from the club over who were also young like me and were more innocent than the first group of girls I hung out with. I think all three of us were curious about what it would be like to kiss another girl, so as the night went on, we began to experiment. Tim was at work, but I thought that when he came home, he would be happy to see me with the other girls getting into it. But he came home drunk, and when he saw us, he stomped into the other room. Confused by his reaction, I followed him. The only reason I had done this in the first place was so that he would be more into me, and now he was mad at me instead. When his temper started to come out, I decided to send the girls home, promising them everything would be okay.

Lost Control

After they left, I quickly went back into the room to figure out what was wrong. I couldn't understand why Tim was so angry. He was the one who encouraged me to do this. I am not sure if it was jealousy or the alcohol, but wow, was he mad! He was scaring me this time. I had never seen him act this way before. Shaking from head to toe, I grabbed the phone to call 911. Before I could, I felt his heavy foot hit my abdomen to stop me from the calling the police, and I fell into our bedroom closet. This was so traumatic, and I can't remember what happened next. It's as if my brain had turned off, like it knew I couldn't handle the pain of the situation, and shut down to protect me. This is true for other traumas I had been through. I don't remember what happened after that or how the fight ended. What I do know is that I did not end the relationship like I should have because I was still there.

I began to question why he was not using protection during sex. Twelve years of Catholic school education didn't teach me much about sex other than abstinence, but I do remember hearing about condoms. This was my first sexual experience, and to say I was clueless was an understatement. I asked him about it, and he told me he was "fixed" and could no longer have children. A few months later, however, he told me he had the procedure reversed and there was a small chance that I could get pregnant. The moment he said that, I felt that I was pregnant. I began to take pregnancy tests, and for the first couple weeks, they all came back negative. Finally, on Mother's Day, what I already knew was confirmed—I was going to be a mommy.

What a wild few months it had been. In September I had lost my virginity, and by May I was pregnant with my first child—and I was only eighteen! We shared the news with my parents, who were skeptical of my relationship, to say the least. That night at dinner, my dad sang, "First comes love, the comes marriage, then comes baby in the baby carriage." He was right; we were doing things way out of order, and that needed to change quickly. It wasn't just about us anymore; we were bringing a baby into this world. A month later, we decided we were going to go to Gatlinburg, Tennessee, to be married.

The Wedding

About a week before we left for Tennessee, there was a hard, persistent knock at our door followed by, "This is the police!" I was scared out of my mind because I had never been in trouble before and was confused by why the police were at our door. They wanted to ask Tim a few questions. Apparently, there were outstanding warrants out for his arrest. Tim stayed cool, calm, and collected. He insisted the cops had confused him with someone else and showed them his driver's license to clear things up. He insisted that his birthdate did not match that of the guy they were looking for. They left. I felt somewhat relieved, because if the cops felt everything was fine, then I guess I should, too—right? Of course, I found out much later that this warrant was actually for him. He was using two different birth dates to throw things off a bit.

So, we moved forward with the wedding and headed to Tennessee. We found a cute little chapel, and I rented a dress because I hadn't brought one with me. The wedding was nice, for the most part. It was certainly not the day I had always imagined, but I had a dress and got my hair done. Looking back, I sometimes wonder what people were thinking when they saw the two of us together, like the lady doing my hair for the wedding. Here I was, this beautiful, nineteen-year-old girl who had her whole life ahead of her, and I had just run off to another city to marry this man almost twice my age. I wonder why she didn't whisper in my ear and say, "Honey, you don't have to do this; you have your whole life ahead of you." I have always tried to look on the bright side of things though. My parents were there, and I remember my dad crying through most of the ceremony. I wasn't sure at the time if he was crying because he was happy or because he was sad. Afterward, when he refused to shake Tim's hand, it became obvious that those tears were not happy tears. We went out for pizza and Putt-Putt golf with my family after the wedding. Most people would not want to go to Pizza Hut for their wedding reception, but it was our reception, so they went with it.

Financial Changes

I guess I really expected everything in our relationship to be different from that moment on, since we were now married. We had rented a cabin for our honeymoon, and I remember lying there in bed next to him, joining our hands together and looking at our rings. These rings were a symbol of forever to me, and just staring at them brought me such peace. Everything still did not feel quite right, but for this night, it was good enough.

We ran out of money in the middle of our time there. We had just started running a little sports memorabilia shop at the local flea market on the weekends, so we called the guy who was taking care of it while we were gone and asked him to wire us some money. Since I was new to "adulting" and Tim didn't seem concerned about it, I wasn't either. The shop was a great distraction for me while I was pregnant.

The stripping job was not going to work out for me for very much longer, as I couldn't hide my pregnancy while being almost completely naked onstage. Some dancers worked their entire pregnancy, and they looked adorable. I knew I wasn't going to be one of those women. I was widening quickly. We would have to depend on Tim's income, which was very unstable. My phone got turned off often, and I would have to use a pay phone to call my mom. When I was working, we lived like celebrities; when I was not, we were barely surviving. We were either eating steak or off the dollar menu at McDonald's. There was no in between.

When Tim and I first moved in together, he had told me about his love for sports memorabilia, so being the pleaser I was, I was into it, too. We had acquired a lot of things and I really started to develop a love for the hobby. The anticipation of opening a pack of baseball cards and having the opportunity to find the latest and greatest card was thrilling. It was so exciting being in the shop every weekend. We never knew who the next customer was going to be.

One weekend, this guy walked into our shop with a rare card he was trying to sell. He said the card was his grandfather's and it was a Babe Ruth tobacco card. During this time, there were a lot of fake cards on the market, and we had no way of knowing if the card was legit or not. Tim said he would be willing to take a chance on it for $20 and, to everyone's surprise, the man agreed. I took the card up to a local authenticator that week to find out if the card was real or not. He studied the card and handed it back to me, telling me that it was, in fact, the real deal. I was so excited to have such a piece of history.

Our shop also helped significantly with our finances. Although we didn't make a ton of money, any extra coming in helped.

The pregnancy went along normally, aside from a few slight complications along the way. I was anemic and had low potassium, so I was often exhausted. I also experienced leg cramps that were absolutely miserable. I had quite a few lightheaded spells and passed out a couple times when my blood was drawn. January finally came, and it was time to have that baby girl.

The labor was long and painful. Eighteen long hours went by, and no epidural. I was tired and wasn't sure I had it in me to finish out the labor process. When I was finally administered the epidural, it made my blood pressure drop and affected the baby's heartbeat dramatically at first. The doctors and nurses were in a frenzy trying to stabilize us. When they felt we were both doing okay, it was now time for me to begin to push. I was exhausted; could I really finish this? I remember yelling at my mom, saying, "Get this baby out of me!" With much perseverance and determination, my beautiful baby girl was finally here. I knew at that very moment every ounce of pain I had experienced was all worth it. As they began to deliver the placenta, which, at the time, I didn't even know was a thing, it hurt so bad I thought I was pushing another baby out. Finally, it was all over, and I could now just bond with my baby. I began to feed her but quickly had to pass her over to my mother. My face grew pale, and I felt like I was going to pass out. I am not sure what was happening at the time, whether it was the loss of blood or just plain exhaustion from all my body endured, but I needed a moment to recover, and I was glad my mom was there to help.

We named our little princess McKenzie Kay, and when I revealed her name to my mom, she began to cry. Kay is my mom's middle name, and she had no idea we were going to name our daughter after her. It was a special moment that I will never forget, seeing the look of surprise on her face.

Chapter 5
Motherhood

Motherhood changed me from the inside out. It was like I had a great awakening. I began to see things I didn't see before. I was not okay with being treated poorly anymore. Maltreatment I had once justified was not going to fly anymore. That baby was beautiful; she was my everything, and she needed me. It was almost like I grew up overnight. Although I had just turned nineteen, I was now a mom with a child who depended on me for everything. While I had no problem justifying pain being inflicted on me, there was no way I was going to let anyone hurt this sweet baby!

After my sweet girl was about a month old, it became very obvious that I needed to get out of this relationship, for the sake of both of us. Tim had a violent temper and made our environment toxic, to say the least. Once, he had gone to Wendy's and brought home food for us. I was so nervous watching him open all the bags to see if they got his order just right. He had ordered a double cheeseburger, which was suppose to have only mustard and lettuce on it. When he checked the food, however, the double cheeseburger had everything on it, and was he pissed! He was so mad, he threw that cheeseburger across the room, and the contents of the burger flew everywhere. I understood being upset about not getting your order right, but his behavior was over the top.

I knew I needed to get out of this situation, so I started making plans to leave him. Tim tried everything he could think of to manipulate us into staying. He threatened that he would take full custody of our daughter if I left. While the thought of that scared me to death, I just knew I had to get out and I wasn't leaving without her. He said he had a lot of connections from when he used to work in the sheriff's office, so he was sure to win in court. Every moment I stayed was putting us both in jeopardy. There was nothing else I could do but leave, no matter the threats.

Back Home

We moved back into my parents' house, and I hired the best lawyer that money could buy. Tim wasn't making much effort to visit the baby though, and he seemed more interested in trying to control me. He threatened to blow up my car, a gift from my parents that was in his possession, and also threatened to harm me. He had lost his power over me, and he knew it. I went to the courthouse and filed for an emergency protection order for my daughter and me. This made me feel a little safer. Once the order expired, he was only allowed to have supervised visitations with the baby once a week. Even though he had limited access to her, I was still terrified every moment she was not with me, worrying if she was okay. He had threatened to take off with her in the past. What if his threats became reality? How could I possibly get through life without her? I hired the best lawyer

I could afford because this was one battle I was not going to lose. McKenzie needed her mom and she needed to be protected, so I was going to do whatever it took to make sure she was.

I starting looking for a job to get my life back in order and to pay for the lawyer. My circumstances had changed so much and I needed to make a lot more money, so I went back to being a stripper. My body had changed since my pregnancy and I wasn't as confident initially, but soon I was back to making a lot of money. It was a good job for a single mom. I was able to spend the entire day with my baby and my mom would put her to sleep right before I'd leave for work. I also started socializing again. One night a week, I would put my baby to sleep and head out dancing with friends. A part of me wanted to feel young again. During the day, my daughter was my world and the bond we had was unbreakable, but at nighttime when she was sleeping, mommy would go play with her friends. It was super weird that I could only get into the "eighteen and up" clubs. I know I was only nineteen, but I certainly didn't feel like all the other teens I was surrounded by.

Strip Club World

Being a part of the strip club world was unlike anything I had ever encountered. I had experienced sexual abuse as a child, rape as an adult, and now more sexual abuse as a stripper. I know what some of you are thinking: I put myself in that position by dancing on a man's lap, practically naked, and you are going to get touched sometimes. I am not

49

blaming you for thinking that way—I have made that same judgement myself. Regardless, customers are expected to follow the rules and touching is not allowed, but, of course, not everyone followed those rules. With every unwanted touch, I fell deeper and deeper into trauma. You have to understand, every time I took off my clothes in that place, I had to somehow trust everyone not to take advantage of me.

Every time I began a lap dance with a new guy, I had to somehow convince myself he was going to follow the rules and not touch me. When they broke that trust and did it anyways, I still had to continue to do my job. We put up boundaries to keep us safe as humans, but when those boundaries are constantly crossed, something happens inside of you that is so damaging. Detrimental thoughts of feeling like I am just an object, not worthy of anything better, try to take over. I was thankful when I turned twenty-one because at least then I was allowed to have a few drinks every night, which allowed me to stuff down the pain inside of me. It became increasingly harder to do that job and deal with the constant abuse, night after night. Honestly, I was as close to being a prostitute as you legally could be, and it disgusted me. I was really a good girl my whole life and now, although I had only had sex with one guy, many guys got off on me or about me. The thought of it made me sick, and no matter how many dances I gave or how long I danced, I was never okay with it. Occasionally, a guy would jump up in the middle of the dance and dart to the restroom, and, in my innocent naivety, I had no idea why.

Never in my life had I imagined that this is what sex would look like when I grew up. Some of the girls seemed okay with it, others even seemed to enjoy it. But it was killing me inside, and I am sure they were hurting, too, they just couldn't express it. I don't think any little girl grows up thinking their value lies in their body or sex. No, I think a lot of these girls were hurt in some way, maybe like I was.

Although the environment was still very competitive, these women became like my family. One of the dancers was always nurturing toward me. She was motherly and a great listener, and she was deeply empathetic toward my life experiences. It felt good to have someone who could relate and cared. A lot of these women knew my history and what I had gone through with Tim. While he no longer worked at that club, there were a few still loyal to him who had a hard time believing anything I said. It was hurtful, but I understood they just wanted to protect a friend. Thankfully, their dislike toward me lessened as time went on, and things became a little more peaceful.

Jerry

When I went out dancing with my friends, the DJ of the club caught my eye. I made it my goal to get his attention. He was playing hard to get, but this was a part of my attention-getting cycle, and I liked the challenge. Eventually, I won, and we began dating. I was having a good time getting to know him and was feeling hopeful about having a whole family someday.

Jerry and I wanted to spend a lot of time together. I wanted to spend all my time with him *and* with my daughter, but I couldn't have it both ways. Jerry lived an hour from my parents' house, which made it difficult to sustain our relationship. I wasn't ready to end it though, so I packed up my daughter and moved out of my parents' house. We lived in an extended stay hotel for about a month, and Jerry would watch the baby at night while I worked. Up until this point, Jerry had refused to tell me his age. It would have been wise to find that information out before I moved into a hotel for this relationship, but I was not thinking with my brain, I was thinking with my heart. He finally told me he was in his forties. I was now twenty. Red flag alert! I thought, *Am I getting back into another bad situation?* Once again, I started to justify the red flags and allowed the relationship to continue.

I found a great townhouse to rent for a year, and Jerry moved in. We lived less than an hour away from my mom, who used to watch the baby while I worked, but now Jerry was the only support I had. While Jerry claimed to have a business, there was no income coming in, and although he watched my daughter while I was working, he did not help pay any of the bills. Again, red flag!

Dark Knight in Shining Armor

Jerry and I dated for a couple of years before I found a letter he was going to mail to the Church of Scientology. The letter revealed that when we first started dating, he had cheated on me (it was a doctrine of this church to confess one's "sins"). I was devastated but didn't really know what to do about it, especially given the position I was in. We talked about it, and he got defensive before shifting the blame onto

52

me and making me feel guilty for finding the letter in the first place. At that point, the relationship became drastically different, and I lost all trust in him.

During one slow night at work, I sat down and talked to a man I'd met named Larkin. I was in a vulnerable position and wanted someone to listen to me and appreciate me. There was immediate chemistry, and for the first time, I gave my phone number to a customer. I had a newfound hope. We talked online and got to know each other that way. I was still with Jerry, but I was falling for Larkin fast. It felt like a fairytale, and I thought he was going to be my knight in shining armor that was going to rescue me from the mess I was in. I decided it was time to leave Jerry and go back home to my parents' house, AGAIN. Jerry didn't take the news well and, to retaliate, took the car I bought that we had put in his name. He called it his "babysitting" money. This was super disheartening since I had paid for everything for the duration of our relationship.

From Stilettos to Grace

Chapter 6
Pursuing Happily Ever After

My relationship with Larkin was different than my previous relationships. Everything felt like a magical fairytale. He was a super Disney fanatic and a serious hopeless romantic. We had watched the movie *Serendipity* and decided that this was our story. I gifted him a glove and I kept the other one. It was a super romantic scene in the movie when the two main characters meet each other while trying to purchase gloves. When they reached to grab the gloves, their hands touched, and they shared an instant chemistry. This is the moment it all began. When things were great in the relationship, they were REALLY great, but when things were bad, he turned into another person and things got REALLY dark. One night in a parking lot where we often met to spend time together, he got very upset and didn't want me to leave. I had decided it was time to go and refused to engage in the conversation any longer. I started to roll up my car window when he decided to spit at me. He then followed behind me as I drove off.

Another time, we were arguing over the phone and I had enough and hung up on him. He called back, but I let it go to voicemail. Then, he called my parents and left a message on their voicemail with a made up a story that I was on drugs. Thankfully, this time that red flag was enough for me to end the relationship, but the threats and pleading for me to come back didn't stop. I ended up going to the police department to file a complaint. This was all getting a bit too scary, and I just wanted to make them aware of the situation in case he totally lost his mind and decided to come after me.

Enough is Enough

I finally decided enough was enough. I was going to break this cycle of bad relationships and focus on myself and my daughter. I was going to stay single until I found a man who met the requirements I was looking for. So, I made a list.

I began to work at Longhorn's Steakhouse as a server and quickly worked my way up to management level. I was starting to make some decent money without my income as an exotic dancer. I was able to give my daughter a nice life and good care and felt I had finally turned the page and things were looking up. I was finally becoming an adult, I thought. I continued to live with my parents, as they were able to help me care for my daughter while I was at work.

About a year later, some friends and I started going to karaoke places after work. It was harmless fun and something I could do after my daughter was already asleep. One night, we tried out a new bar/restaurant called HooHas. We were having a good time listening to others sing while we waited for our turn to come up on the list. Suddenly, a man walked up to sing with a voice unlike any other I had heard before. It took my breath away! Immediately, all eyes were drawn to this man belting out "Welcome to the Jungle." I had never heard someone hit such high notes before, and wow, was I blown away! I was immediately attracted. One of the qualities I included on my list for the guy I wanted to fall in love with was that he would be an amazing singer. We started visiting this bar often, and it quickly became our new hot spot. I even went there for lunch one day with a friend, just hoping to see this mystery man again. It wasn't long before my friend let the cat out of the bag to this man that I was crushing on him hard. Later, I found out that my friend told this guy to tell me he was too good for me. I was horrified!

I discovered this mystery cutie was part owner of HooHas. So, I planned to stop by there as much as possible. One day, I stopped in for lunch and saw him playing darts with the other owner. The daytime crowd wasn't as lively, and when I walked in, he noticed me. I remember I was wearing this hot pink tank. He made it a point to get to know me, and this relationship moved just as fast as my previous ones. I am the type of girl that falls hard and fast. He, however, was different. He was a nice guy and checked almost all my boxes.

His name was George, and again, he was much older than I was, but was a big kid at heart. He was playful and kind. I introduced him to my daughter and they both immediately fell for one another. He let her get away with everything and got her anything her heart desired. Six months later, we were engaged and married within the year. I finally had my dream fairytale wedding and felt that I had truly found "the one." I was dressed like a princess for the big day and felt like one, too. He was handsome and looked like a prince. It seemed I was going to get my "happily ever after," after all.

Faith and Frustration

The marriage was going great. It finally felt like I had a real family. You know the ones you see on television as a child and expect that your family will look like that someday. Mom, Dad, and Baby. In my case, McKenzie wasn't a baby anymore, she was seven, but I happily overlooked these details knowing that I finally had a complete family. George adored McKenzie. He was in his forties and had never been a dad before. He was having the time of his life experiencing fatherhood for the first time. The only problem with their relationship is that he had no boundaries—she could get whatever she wanted from him. He could not tell my sweet girl no. It was hard, sometimes, always having to be the bad guy, but I felt so blessed to be married to a man who loved my daughter as much as I did.

We started a multi-level marketing business together and attended many seminars. We even began to entertain the idea of faith. Although the business wasn't bringing in a bunch of money, the principles we were taught were outstanding. We heard about God at these conferences in a way we had never heard before. The leadership team really seemed to have a relationship with God, and it even sounded like they heard from Him. I grew up in the Catholic faith and hadn't really heard people talk in this way before. I had never imagined having a relationship with God was really a thing.

I guess I thought that was the priest's job. George and I never really talked about God, and neither one of us was even sure He existed.

John, our mentor from the MLM business, invited us to church. We agreed to go because we respected and trusted his recommendation. Also, the seeds planted in the seminars we had been attending began to soften my heart toward God. You see, when I was young, I loved God, but I think I was more afraid of Him than anything else. I tried to be a "good girl" so someday I could get to heaven. I think I gave up on Him, though, when bad things continued happening in my life. I wondered, "How can God be real and not protect me from all this?" But as I continued to hear about this God they knew, I become more and more intrigued.

We really started to enjoy going to church and began attending almost every Sunday. We'd go to the morning service together, but if George had to work, McKenzie and I would go to the evening service. I started feeling something I had never felt before in my life. I believed in Christ once again. One evening toward the end of the service, the pastor gave what they call an "altar call." As I heard the music and listened to what was being said, something inside of me urged me to go forward. I made my way down to the altar with McKenzie in tow. Standing there, I didn't really know what to do, but I knew this was the moment I truly believed; the moment of my salvation, when I came into relationship with Christ Jesus. Things started to change from there, and being an "all or nothing at all" kind of girl, I went all in.

Confusing Symptoms

George and I were married in May but by January of the following year, he became sick. He was so sick! He was also constantly exhausted. After going to the doctor, he was diagnosed with the flu. I was so relieved to have an answer as to why he felt so terrible, but as days and weeks went by, he seemed to get only worse. Other strange symptoms appeared. Lumps formed all over his body. We were so confused.

I had bought my mom a trip for her birthday that included an overnight stay at the casino. We were looking forward to it, and George assured us he would be okay to go ahead as planned. He had a doctor's appointment scheduled for the following day at a specialist to get a hernia looked at. By the time he got to the doctor's office, he was as pale as a ghost and vomiting. They did some blood work on him and found an abnormality in his white blood cell count, so they sent him straight to the hospital. My mom and I were at breakfast at the casino when he called me, crying and scared, saying he was on his way to the hospital. We grabbed the check and headed out the door in a hurry to get to the hospital as fast as possible. When we showed up, he had calmed down a bit but was still scared. Even though he was shaken up, he was still my silly George.

We called family to let them know he was at the hospital, but I still didn't know what was going on with him. The hospital staff would only tell us that he was "a very sick man." I was getting beyond frustrated. They made it sound like he was knocking on death's door but would not give me any answers as to what was wrong with him. Finally, a doctor came in and shut the door behind him. Nothing could have prepared me for the words he spoke to us next. He started in the same way, saying George was very ill, and followed that with, "He has leukemia." More specifically, he believed it was AML-Acute Myeloid Leukemia, a type of cancer of the blood and bone marrow that interferes with the production of normal white blood cells. He told us that AML progresses aggressively and that the best chance George would have at surviving would be to get transferred to Jewish Hospital in Ohio.

There, they had a specific floor and doctors dedicated to caring for aggressive cancers, with treatments like chemotherapy, drug therapies, and stem-cell transplants. The news shocked us, and all we could do was cry. The doctor gave us some hope by saying that because George was young enough and strong, he had a good chance to beat it. We were ready right then to go to the other hospital immediately and fight this thing, but unfortunately, they did not have a room available that night, so we spent the night in the ICU.

Facing the Nightmare

That night, we asked many questions and tried to stay hopeful. I was in shock but still reaching out for answers to understand how this had happened to my husband. I knew what was wrong with him. He had leukemia. The doctor told me that already, but it just hadn't sunk in. We ate dinner and had some visitors, trying to stay positive, but the truth was, I had never been so scared in my entire life. Everything I knew was about to change forever. Lying there that night, I didn't know if George would even wake up the next morning. I even vaguely remember a nurse crying as she came in to check on us. This was too much to handle. But we had no choice. We would have to face reality again in the morning. That night, I prayed I would wake up and find that this was all just a nightmare. I woke up and it was still reality. So, it was time to face it.

The ambulance arrived that morning and we began the transportation process to Jewish Hospital. The doctor felt that George was too sick to be transported any other way but in an ambulance with a team of people to support him, if needed. So, we got into the ambulance. It was the first time I had ever ridden in an ambulance. We tried to make small talk, but every person we chatted with since George entered the hospital had a different look on their face that, up until that point in my life, I was unfamiliar with. They looked at us with pity and almost hopelessness. Like they felt what we must be feeling, too. I pride myself that one of my biggest strengths was being optimistic. I can't live in a state of hopelessness for long. I can almost always find the good in every situation. But in this situation, I was struggling to find hope, and it didn't help that George's caregivers didn't seem to have much hope either.

Eventually, we found our strength that day. We arrived at Jewish Hospital, where the staff seemed unfazed by our situation, given that they saw cases like this every day. George's personal team of doctors met with us to assess his situation. They looked over the charts from the other hospital, asked us some questions, and came ready with a plan. They wanted to use George's case for a clinical trial and follow his progress. This was scary to me, and I wasn't sure I wanted my husband to be a guinea pig. I asked the doctor his advice, and he assured me George's treatment options would be the same, trial or not, so I felt more confident agreeing.

Everything went so fast that day. George had to get some testing done to make sure his major organs could handle the amount of poison they were about to inject into him. They had to give him a bone marrow biopsy, which was an awful procedure to watch, and I can't imagine what it felt like. The doctor collected bone fragments from his back side by major force with a tool that screwed into the bone and grinded out fragments for testing. I could hear the grinding of the bone as George cried out in agony. He also had a port put into his chest, which made it easier to administer medicine and saved him from being poked for blood over and over again. George was awake for each of these procedures, and the pain he had to endure that first day was insane.

That day, we also learned that George would be in the hospital for a minimum of thirty days and my daughter would not be allowed into the unit to visit him. He was heartbroken. I was heartbroken. My parents cared for her during that time. George was knocking on death's door almost every day, and although I wanted to be there for my daughter, I felt that no one should have to go through what he was going through alone. My parents were perfectly able to take care of McKenzie, and she was comfortable with them, so that made the decision much easier.

A new day began, and it was time to hear the results of tests and when the chemo would begin. The team of doctors made their rounds and came ready with details. They confirmed the diagnosis from the bone marrow biopsy and said George was ready to go for chemo. In fact, they wanted to administer his first dose that same day. It was all moving so quickly, but we were beginning to have more hope because of the knowledge this team brought to the table.

Chapter 7
Hanging on to Hope

It was chemo time. I don't know what I was expecting, but I think I was expecting a more dramatic event as they came in to do the chemo. They brought a bag of chemo in and sat with us while it flowed into his body. We all chatted like everything was totally normal. A little bit of normal during this time was a nice break from reality, though. The drama did come shortly after George's first dose of chemo, unfortunately. He began to shake uncontrollably and was freezing. I was very concerned as I ran to get more blankets. On the other hand, the nurses did not seem worried and assured me that it was just chemo chills. We brought in lots of blankets and tried to warm him up, but he kept shaking, almost like he was having a seizure. Finally, a nurse came in and pushed the "code" button before making us leave the room. In the waiting room, I began to cry uncontrollably as I watched a team of doctors and nurses run to my husband's room. I honestly thought that was it. The only other time I had experienced that before was with my grandfather, and they were not able to revive him. I cried and cried and prayed and prayed as I waited for answers. Finally, a team came in and told us they were able to stabilize the situation but had to put George on a ventilator. I was terrified again. Almost every person I knew that was put on a ventilator died. They were still going to continue with the chemo while he was on the ventilator. The thought of what the next day would bring scared me. Visitors were in and out that day, and if George ever opened his eyes for a minute, he wanted the tube out of his mouth and said he was thirsty. Honestly, it was better for him to be asleep through this time. A few days had passed, and the chemo treatments seemed to be going okay. There was even talk of him coming off the ventilator soon.

It was January 20, 2008, and it was my daughter's 7th birthday. I asked the nurses to keep the date off of the whiteboard so George didn't wake up and realize what day it was and what he was missing. His sister came over to sit with him for a few hours and I snuck off to Chuck E. Cheese to have a small party to celebrate McKenzie's birthday. It was the first time I had left the hospital other than for a smoke break since this whole thing had started. I was so nervous something was going to happen while I was gone that I was barely present. I wanted to soak in all the sweet time with my daughter that I could, but it was so hard to stay focused. She was so excited for her birthday party, and her grandma had made her a beautiful barbie doll cake. She felt like a little princess. We finished up our time at the party, and I headed back to the hospital. Thoughts filled my mind of all the things that could have happened while I was away from George.

I returned to find all was well at the hospital, and we ended the day snuggled up together on the bed. He did not like it when I left his side. H always noticed when I was gone. Sometimes, when I took a smoke break and had two cigarettes instead of one, he would notice I was gone a little longer than he expected. He was scared, I'm sure; I know I was. The ventilator came out, and we finished up our thirty day stay. The doctors were confident the treatment had worked and the leukemia was gone. George's numbers dropped really low and they were climbing back up again nicely, so the doctors felt it was okay to send him home. We would come back in a week or so for another biopsy to make sure that the leukemia was truly gone.

Thoughts of Eternity

After George was taken off the ventilator, it became a very real thing for me, I mean, where George would spend eternity. He had started going to church with us, but he still was not sold on the idea of salvation and God yet. A couple of church members had come by to talk to us, but it never seemed like it was the right time, and George was not interested in talking to them. However, there was this young pastor at the church we were attending that George did like; he had heard him preach once and met him at a Halloween "trunk or treat" the church was hosting. His name was Andre, and he was blowing up balloon animals when we had stopped to talk to him for a while. George was just a big kid at heart, so Andre's youthful nature made him likable and relatable to George. I contacted Andre and asked if he would talk to George about salvation. When he arrived, I left the room and gave them some time alone. After a while,

Andre walked into the hallway with a huge smile on his face. He told me they had prayed together and that George asked Jesus into his life. I was so relieved! No matter what happened now, I would see George in heaven someday.

George's attitude after that experience changed. One day, "Live Like You Were Dying" by Tim McGraw came on the radio, and George scooted his way off the bed. He didn't have much strength, but he grabbed me by the hand, and there in that hospital room, we slow danced. The lyrics had never been more relevant than they were now. I had probably heard that song a hundred times before and never really thought about the meaning, but as we faced this very real life or death situation, we both knew exactly what the song meant now. It was one of those moments where neither of us had to say a word. Both of our hearts knew and were connected.

We went home with lots of hope. We felt that George had beaten this, and we praised God for healing him. We were sure this battle had been won, and George seemed to be getting stronger every day. When we returned for George's follow up appointment, we walked back into the hospital more confident than ever. We honestly felt sorry for the other people being treated there because they were still fighting the battle and George had won his. Boy, did we get a wakeup call! He went back for another bone marrow biopsy. Thankfully, they gave him a stronger medication and he handled the biopsy well. I don't think I will ever forget that terrible sound of cranking and grinding of bone. Nothing could prepare us for what we heard next.

Wake Up Call

We were in this tiny room when the doctor came in and closed the door behind him. He had that look in his eye, and I knew things were not okay. He said the leukemia was back. We were in shock!

"What do you mean it is back?" I questioned. "George just beat it." The doctor sat with us for a while, helping us process our questions and concerns. We were not without hope though, as he presented another plan. George would need to be admitted to the hospital for another thirty days, and once his numbers were low enough, they would give him a bone marrow transplant. They wanted to check if his sisters were a match, but if not, he would be put on the bone marrow transplant list. One of his sisters said no, but the other went in for testing right away. She was a close enough match, so we were able to proceed as planned.

The hospital became our new home. We even requested certain rooms and our favorite nurses. The nurses became my best friends and chatting with them helped me feel somewhat normal. Sometimes, the weekend doctors bought lunch for the nurses, and they would come by to see what I wanted and sneak my order in. They took care of me and George. I was not the patient, but I sure needed support during this time in my life. George counted on me to be his strength and help take care of him. I was glad to do so—I was willing to do anything I could do to help.

The time had come for the transplant. George's numbers were pretty much bottomed out and everything was a go. His sister arrived at the hospital for her part. She became my new hero, and the words "thank you" did not seem big enough. They got what they needed from her, and she recovered well after her surgery. Then, they transported what George needed upstairs. I was surprised by how unfazed the doctors and nurses were. For me, this was a big event, but for George's part, they just came in and hung up a bag, and we all watched its contents go into his system through his port. Everything went smoothly, thankfully, and the rest of the day was pretty calm. The process was easy for George, but we were warned about everything that could occur as the days and weeks went on. They told us that at any time, George's body could start rejecting the transplanted bone marrow, which would worsen his condition quickly. The threat of that circled around in my head as the days went by, but we tried to remain hopeful.

Rollercoaster

Everything was going well, and once again, the doctors were confident George's leukemia was gone. We finally felt like the battle had been won—again. We went home, and as George began to regain his strength, we tried to go on with life as normally as possible. Little did we know only a few weeks later we would find ourselves back at the emergency room at Jewish Hospital.

We felt so defeated! When would this rollercoaster end? However, we were happy that he was still on the ride to begin with.

The devastating news came back—the cancer had spread to his brain. It was as though the air had been sucked out of us. We were drained of nearly every last bit of encouragement. The team, however, had a plan. They were going to install a port into George's head to access the cancer directly. This process was significantly different than our previous experiences so far. It was kind of crazy to watch them inject medicine into his head. I had never seen anything like it. The treatment went along well, for the most part, until George started getting horrible headaches. I mean, not just your typical migraines; these headaches were taking him down. They ran some CT scans, provided some medications to alleviate his pain, and even tried a caffeine IV treatment. I volunteered to sign up for the caffeine treatments, too! Seriously, I was tired. They wouldn't share with me though.

God, Give Me the Words...

Nothing they tried relieved George's headaches. He was in so much pain, and my concern and anxiety were growing. I wanted the doctors to run an MRI, but they didn't think it was necessary and believed it would be an incredibly uncomfortable experience for George. I wanted to find out what was wrong to fix whatever was hurting, and although George's doctors weren't listening, I did not give up. I felt God was helping me fight this battle.

One evening got really weird and crazy. I was so scared that I didn't know what to do. George turned into a different person. He started to question me about everything and didn't trust anything I said. He didn't know where he was and seemed to be losing it. Enough was enough. I pleaded with God that night to give me the right words to say so George could get the MRI he needed. I was so scared and wept until I fell asleep. The next morning came, and usually I was awake before the doctors made their rounds in the morning, but this morning, I wasn't fully awake yet as I listened to the typical news they had. When it came time for me to ask questions, I believe God gave me the words to say. I reminded the doctors of an earlier issue George had with his sinuses. If this was causing his headaches, we could possibly treat the problem the same way. I recommended they do an MRI, and they finally said YES! At that moment, I felt like I had won the lottery. After days and countless conversations, they were finally doing an MRI. I knew it was God because my own efforts had always failed.

They scheduled the MRI, and although it was going to be a difficult process, I was ready for it. Thankfully, George seemed to like me again and wanted me nearby. At one point, they had to stop the MRI because he started to freak out, and I had to go in with him to soothe him. He made it through; the doctors got the pictures they needed and we were on the way. Well, kind of on the way. After testing, we waited in the hallway for transportation back to George's room, which took forever. When our transportation arrived, we were instead brought to the ICU, as the MRI had revealed that George had a bleed in his brain.

The news was a shock. I had no idea what it meant other than it was not good, but the doctors had a plan to reduce the bleeding.

But by the next day it was a different story. The color of George's skin began to turn ashen gray. I was no expert, but I knew skin turning gray was not a good thing. I grew very concerned. Their plan now was to perform a "burr hole" surgery. This surgery was very risky, and there was a high chance that George would die on the table, they said. I was terrified, but it was our only option. If he didn't have the surgery, he would surely die. He was in a grave state, but at least this surgery gave him a chance.

I signed the consent form for the surgery because George was not coherent enough to do so. When I signed that paper and read about the risk this surgery held, I felt as though I had just signed my husband's life away. The whole situation felt surreal. I called family and friends in to visit him due to the extreme nature of the surgery. This visit may have possibly been their final goodbye to George. Family came throughout the day and there were a lot of tears shed. When all the goodbyes were said, they prepared George for surgery.

Facing It

The time had come that I was looking forward to and terrified of. I stood silently while the transport team prepared George's bed to roll him to surgery. I was not going to leave his side until they made me. I walked with him and held his hand as he rolled down the long hall to surgery. He was barely conscious, but as we went, I explained to him the surgery he was about to have and that it was risky, but I reassured him that I believed he was going to be okay. I told him again that he had a bleed in his brain (subdural hematoma) and that the surgery would relieve the pressure so he could start feeling better. I calmly explained that they would drill a small hole in his head to release the excess blood. I wanted to be strong for him. I knew if he had hope, he would fight. I kissed George goodbye and watched as the door closed behind him. Then, I absolutely lost it. The minister lady I had become close with was there, and she showed me to an empty room where I could cry and scream away from everyone. She stood with me while I became a complete mess. After a few moments, I pulled it together and looked on the hopeful side of things. I am sure that sweet minister lady ushered peace into that room.

The surgery seemed to take forever, but it probably was only a couple of hours. I was having a hard time sitting in the waiting room as the people around us lived life. This used to irritate me. People around me would start laughing, and I couldn't understand what could be so funny at a time like this. I know that laughter is a good, healthy way to deal with stress, but I couldn't find anything funny in all this and hated the sound of laughter.

Chapter 8
Living for Every Moment

The long wait was finally over when I was called into a small room where the doctor met me. He was pleasantly surprised and excited to share the news that George's surgery had been a success. He told me that the minute he drilled into George's head, a rocket of blood hit the ceiling. He had never seen so much blood launch out of someone's head so quickly. The surgery was the right call and had he not had it, George would have certainly passed away. He mentioned that George was still bleeding, and they installed a drain until the fluid ran clear. I was beyond thankful to him and to the Lord for helping George make it through this dangerous surgery.

George was a rockstar and started to recover quickly. So quickly, in fact, that within a few short days, he was transferred out of the ICU! His transfer couldn't have happened on a better day. It was May 19, 2008, our one-year wedding anniversary. George's move to a regular room was such an amazing gift. We found a movie from the hallway library and watched it together, lying in a regular bed in a regular room. The doctor even approved me to order takeout food from The Cheesecake Factory for our anniversary dinner. This may not seem like a big deal to most, but it was huge for us. During George's hospitalization, his numbers were so low he had to eat prepackaged food to mitigate the risk of exposing his body to germs or infections. George ate nothing but microwavable frozen dinners. Sometimes he was allowed boxes of Mike and Ike's candy, which he loved, but no real food. Not today though. Today, we got to eat real, freshly prepared, yummy food. It was almost like having a home cooked meal, one of the things we missed so much.

Living Like You're Dying

We received the good news that we were able to go home. George's numbers and scans looked good enough, and it seemed that he had once again beaten leukemia. We were cautiously excited though. It really didn't mean anything to us at that point, but we were eager to go home and spend lots of time with McKenzie. Being away from her had been difficult. Although McKenzie loved spending time with my parents, we missed her, and she missed us. There was no place like home, and all of us together felt like home. We took advantage of every second we had together because we never knew how long it was going to last. We watched lots of movies and had friends and family over for visits.

One day, we went out to do some Putt-Putt golfing with McKenzie and our parents. At this point, we were living like we were dying. We were wise to take advantage of every moment we had together. It was a scorcher of a day, and we had to take a break on a nearby bench when George started to feel weak. By the time we sat down, however, it was too late and he passed out. George's stature had changed so significantly by then that I was able to scoop him up in my arms and get him inside where there was air conditioning. Have you ever experienced a trauma so intense that others can't help but react? My adrenaline kicked in and I didn't have time to feel anything about the situation. Others around us saw the severity of the situation and came to our aid. Someone called 911, and others brought cold towels and water. Slowly, George came around and was stabilized. The concerned looks on people's faces made me realize how normalized this situation had become for me.

The handsome, strong man I married had become a frail, helpless man and was sicker than I even realized. The EMS team looked at me and had more questions than answers. They asked, "What happened to him?" and "Why does he look this way?" rather than, "Why are you here?" George was bald from the treatment and had a dome on top of his head covered over with skin, which was his chemo port. He was basically skin and bones now, pale as a ghost, and his mouth stayed drooped open because of the cancer in his brain. He sometimes needed to cup his chin to aid himself in talking or chewing. I couldn't see all these things because I was madly in love with him and fighting for his life right along with him. I saw a strong man who took everything that was thrown at him and still wanted to live. I saw a man who still cracked jokes even though he was going through hell on earth. I saw a man who was doing whatever it took to stay here for his family. I explained to the kind EMS workers that George had AML and that we were currently out of the hospital. I also told them that as long as he was stable, we weren't going back to the hospital because there wasn't really anything they could do for him, anyways.

Hoping

Unfortunately, I am not sure what happened to the rest of that day. Trauma steals a lot of memories that way. I do know almost every day since the leukemia diagnosis I woke up with a feeling of disbelief. *Is this real life?* I thought. *Was this all just a nightmare I was going to wake up from? How could I have finally found a man who was so good to me and my daughter and now this was our life?* Of course, I topped it with my usual, God-given positive emotions. He knew I would need positivity to survive. I threw some hope on top of all the darkness, joy, and faith. With hope, I was able to keep moving forward and survive this nightmare. I had unfortunately learned from other traumas in my life that I thrived in emergency situations. I was able to walk in the emergency and make the impossible look possible because with God, there is always a way. Even when people told me there was no way and doom and gloom tried to overtake us, I fought the negativity with my faith in God and brought us back to a hopeful place. Having light in the darkest of places is like breath in your lungs. Without hope and light, darkness will prevail and your desire to live will leave.

We continued to cherish our time together as a little family, but, unfortunately, that time came to an end too soon and we were back at the hospital. The leukemia had once again come back. Our treatment options were limited, but the team at Jewish Hospital was amazing and they didn't want to give up. We were family to them now, and they were fighting for George to live, too. In fact, this had been a part of my battle strategy. I had brought in our wedding album and showed them George and his personality before leukemia took a hold of him. I didn't want them seeing him as just another patient, but instead as a man who was full of life and who had a family that loved him dearly.

Aggressive New Treatment

George began a new aggressive treatment plan that aimed to kill every good and bad cell in his body, nearly taking him to the point of death. The team worked hard and knew how to handle this type of treatment, and George did great, for the most part. But something was different this time. The doctors started dropping hints and sending hospice care staff to talk to us. At the time, we were still full of hope, and we didn't understand why they were talking to us. Had the doctors given up hope? George's treatment team set up a meeting with us to discuss his progress. This had never happened before, and I was concerned. The time for the meeting came and I, of course, was prepared with my questions. I do not remember exactly what I asked, but I went into the meeting full of hope, wanting only answers. When I entered the room, however, it didn't look like a room full of hope. I quickly realized it was time to brace myself, but I was still going to battle against anything that said there was no hope.

The team reviewed all the treatments they had tried so far as they tried to prepare me for the worst; they knew I was still hopeful that we could beat this thing. They started to say things like, "You need to make sure you update your living will and seriously consider your options," and "If George were to have an emergency situation in the hospital, we might not recommend reviving him as he would likely die shortly afterward and be miserable for the rest of his life." They brought up hospice care and the different options they could offer us. I was only half listening as I waited for the option of hope. I thought, *Okay, we have heard this before, but what are you going to do to try to save him?* Those options never came, and I felt like I couldn't breathe.

I left the room crying and trying to figure out how I was going to tell George how the meeting went. I wanted to break the news in a more hopeful way than "You are dying, and you can die here, or in hospice, or at home with hospice. Which one sounds better?" I took a smoke break to pull myself together and process everything before I went back into the room. The time had come for me to put my "big girl pants" on and have one of the hardest conversations of my life. I slowly walked through the long hospital halls and up to George's floor before entering the unit. I took my time as I washed my hands. Usually, I was rushing to get back to him because George did not like to be alone for a long time.

As soon as I entered the room, he wanted to know how the meeting went right away. I sat on the bed and began to give him the information I had just received in the most tender, hopeful way I possibly could. We thumbed through the pamphlet detailing available hospice services, and the messages within the document gave us a little spark of hope. We reached out to the hospice in our state to set up a meeting to learn more details and make an informed decision.

Hospice Choices

Just the act of calling the hospice for a meeting was dark and depressing, but it seemed like our only option. There weren't many choices, and this certainly was not what we were hoping for, but George had already decided he wanted to go home and be with McKenzie. So, once again, we headed home. This time it was very different. This time, the nurses came and said their goodbyes. Though we didn't dare say it, we all knew this would be the last time they would say goodbye. I know a lot of people are ready to bust out of the hospital as quickly as possible, and we were ready for that as well, but this team of people had become our best friends. They had been there for us more than anyone. They had loved and cared for us in the darkest time of our lives.

When we left, we picked McKenzie up from school early, as we didn't want to waste any time we could spend with her. She was excited and surprised. We told my parents the news but didn't want to tell her in case something drastically changed. We were so excited to see her and squeeze her, but underneath all that joy was the heartache of knowing something she didn't that we would have to eventually reveal. We wanted to tell her quickly because we didn't know how much time George had left.

When we got home, we tearfully started talking to her. We tried to be strong, but we shed more tears than we had hoped to. We told her the doctors said Daddy was going to die and that they couldn't help him anymore. Daddy wanted to come home and spend as much time with her as he possibly could. That sweet girl did not like to be left without hope either, so we told her we believed God was in control and had hope that He could still heal him. I am not sure we handled it perfectly, but we handled it the best way we could. I was a twenty-seven-year-old woman who had had harder conversations in the past year than some would ever have in their whole life. We prepared her the best way we could.

Chapter 9
Day by Day

George was home but was still very sick, so we took things one day at a time. He didn't have much of an appetite and I often tried to force him to eat. I had read so much about the process of dying that every sign made me a nervous wreck. My mom brought us cantaloupe, and he really took a liking to that. I was thrilled that he was at least eating something.

One night, things changed drastically. George had an upset stomach, and we went to bed early. I was so exhausted from a lack of sleep that I didn't even notice he had gotten up in the middle of the night without me. He was nauseous through the night and by morning, he decided he had had enough, and it was time to call hospice in. So, I went into my parents' formal living room and made the call I never thought I would have to make.

The hospice staff greeted me with empathy and helped me, as I am sure I cried my whole way through that call. Hospice got the process rolling quickly. Time is limited with many hospice patients, so they sent someone right out. They reviewed the process with us and ordered the items we would need, including a hospital bed we could set up in the living room and everything necessary for George's comfort when he was bedridden. They also provided the medication he needed for a comfortable transition into death, and I was trained on how to administer the drugs into his port if a problem arose.

I called our family and a few close friends to let them know George's decision to call in hospice and that he might only have a few days left.

I had to pick up McKenzie from school and during this time, I gave George some time with his best friend. I told him to help George write a letter to McKenzie so she would have something to remember him by. I waited for them to finish up and brought Kenzie home to a house overcome by hopelessness. By that night, the hospital bed was delivered, and we were set up with a mini hospital right in the living room. George's health had declined drastically during the day and by nightfall, he was completely bedridden. We called in our pastor and his wife, who were now some of our closest friends, to perform a ceremony similar to a last rites. They blessed him with oil, read some beautiful Scriptures, and said a beautiful prayer. By the end of the evening, I walked around the house like a zombie. I was exhausted, confused, overwhelmed, and worst of all, hopeless.

Losing

As I lied down next to George in his hospital bed, I became very aware of his breathing. Unlike our time in the hospital, I was the only one checking on him now. As he slept, I wept silently. We were at the end, and I wasn't ready for it. Thankfully, there was no urgency to say certain things to him before he passed away—well, except for one thing. Over the past eight months, we'd had a lot of difficult conversations. He told me things like, "If I die, I want you to get married again right away, like, within the first year." Of course, I told him no way that was going to happen. We both were very aware how much each one of us loved each other. As I lay there that evening with my head on his chest, I started to realize all the things that he wasn't going to make it to. We had hoped he would be able to celebrate one more Christmas. Well, it was only September and no way now was that going to happen. I began weeping at the thought of my daughter losing another opportunity of having a father. When you bring a child into the world, you hope that you can protect them from major traumas. This time there was nothing I could do to protect her though; her life was going to be instantly different. I began to grieve the loss of a second husband. When we took our wedding vows, I never could have imagined till death do us part was only going to be only sixteen months later. I couldn't even imagine how I was going to go on afterwards. I would drift in and out of sleep that night, maybe for an hour total. I didn't want to sleep. Every second and minute was important at this point, and I didn't want to miss a thing.

Goodbyes

Morning came and with it so did more signs that death was among us. He was completely unable to get up at this point. I had to help him use the restroom at the bed. He was asleep for long periods of time. He was not eating or drinking. He was also turning a grayish color. Family and friends were in and out all day long. I would hear laughter as I sat by his bedside, and I just remember fuming on the inside. I couldn't understand what could be so funny at this point. I know now that all people handle things differently and people cope the way they need to, to survive. But at the time I couldn't stand it. I stared at him and wouldn't leave his side. I was waiting for any sign. If he woke up, I wanted to lock eyes with him first. Time was slipping away from us. Later that afternoon his body began to heat up with a fever. I tried to give him some liquid Tylenol but due to his current state he wasn't able to get that down correctly.

People started to thin out and person after person came up to say their goodbyes to George. George was sleeping but it was very obvious to everyone that this would probably be the last time they were able to say goodbye. I watched and I cried and watched and cried. I couldn't believe this was happening; it was not supposed to end this way.

The pastor's wife, whose name is Charlotte, offered to stay with us that night. She also happened to be a nurse and I guess could see that the end was near, and offered to help. I gladly took her up on the offer as I wanted anyone with any medical knowledge to be able to assist me in caring for him. Charlotte also had become such a good friend that she was like my spiritual doctor that night. Since George had not been waking up anymore, we all decided to take shifts by his side to sleep for an hour or so, so that we could all catch at least a couple of hours of sleep that night. It was my mom, sister, Charlotte, and me on duty that night. It was just me the night before and I was running on about an hour of sleep. At midnight or so before we had started our shifts, George sat up straight in the bed and shouted out loud, "LOVE!" I knew that he was scared, and I told him I loved him, too, and comforted him. He went out again. This was the last words George ever spoke. At that moment I sensed that he was hanging on and waiting for me to tell him it was okay to let go. This was the one talk that we hadn't had, and I was pretty convicted to not have. We were fighters and I didn't want to tell him to stop now but at this point it wasn't about what I wanted at all anymore. He fought so hard and was ready to go, rightfully so, and I was going to let him go in peace.

I made everyone clear out so I could say one of the hardest things of my life. I told him how much I loved him and that McKenzie and I would be okay and that it was time for him to go. I went outside so I could sob loudly without him hearing me and have a smoke. I chatted with Charlotte that night about funeral arrangements and things that I wanted there to celebrate George. I caught an hour of sleep probably around 3 a.m., my sister took a shift by George's side, and I slept for about an hour. When I woke up, I could tell by the look in my sister's eyes that things were not good and the end was near. George's breathing had changed significantly, and the death breathing began. It sounded almost like a loud snore. There were a couple breaths, and then nothing. We all looked at each other like, *Is that it?* And then moments later, there were another few breaths. I gave George a dose of his morphine because I didn't want him to feel any pain as he died. We all waited on edge, knowing his last breath would come at any moment. He breathed like this for two hours. No one slept as we sat with him, and finally, the inevitable happened. George took his last breath here on earth. It was so surreal. I waited and waited, expecting to hear another breath, but nothing came. I took off his oxygen mask, turned off the machine, and cried.

Deep Grief

After a moment of deep grief, things had to start moving again. Hospice was notified to handle the death certificate, and the funeral home was called to take care of George's body. I began to call his family and friends. Each one knew why I was calling as soon as they saw my name on the caller ID. Thankfully, I didn't need to say many words because I didn't have them. I only had tears. I still had to have the hardest talk though, and somehow, I had to find a little more strength to do it. I had to tell my angel sleeping upstairs that her dad had died and let her decide if she wanted to say goodbye. When my grandfather died when I was younger, I deeply struggled with knowing that I never had the chance to say goodbye.

When I made it up the stairs and into her room, McKenzie was sleeping. I knew I was about to awaken this pure and innocent child to one of the biggest traumas in her life and there was nothing I could do to change it. All I could do from this moment forward was to be honest with her and comfort her the best I could through my own grief. She was sleeping in my parents' bed—the same place I ran to after the trauma of my sexual abuse occurred.

I woke McKenzie up and sat with her as calm as I could to relay the news. With tears falling from my eyes, I told her that her dad had passed away. She asked questions like, "what does that mean?" I had to explain that we would never see her dad again on this earth and that he had left his body and went to heaven. I did the best I could to explain death to my innocent, seven-year-old child, but let's be honest, death is tragic and sad. As Christians, we can have hope knowing this is only a temporary end and that we will be joined in heaven together one day, but to a child, that day seems too far away to see as hopeful. McKenzie was a smart kid; she understood what I was telling her and handled the news well. I told her that his body was still in the house and asked if she wanted to say goodbye. I made sure she knew there was no right or wrong answer and that whatever she wanted to do was okay. At first, she decided to stay in bed and watch some SpongeBob, one of her favorite shows. Shortly after, however, she decided she wanted to come downstairs. My heart could hardly handle the goodbye that was about to take place.

McKenzie finally had a father who loved her so deeply, and now he was gone. She crawled up next to him and cried. She asked questions about his body lying there, and through my tears I answered the best I could. Nothing about that day was easy. People came and went to say their final goodbyes. Another difficult moments was about to take place, and to say I wasn't ready for it was an understatement.

From Stilettos to Grace

Chapter 10
Letting Go

The funeral home was on the way with the hearse to remove my sweet husband's body. I couldn't breathe. I had been in this fight with him from the beginning to the end. I never left his side for long, always running back and forth to grab a smoke, food, a shower, or use the bathroom. I needed him and he needed me. He was gone now, and I knew we couldn't keep his body in the house forever, but I couldn't let go. When the hearse arrived, I remained cuddled up next to him for as long as possible to talk to him and say goodbye. I hugged and kissed him before running out of the room. I couldn't watch as they rolled his body out. My heart couldn't take it. I ran to the stairwell but stopped short and turned around. I didn't want to look, but I couldn't not look one last time. I sobbed as they wheeled him out. His body was covered, and he was officially gone. They lifted the stretcher where his frail body laid into the back of the hearse and off they went, down the rolling hills of my parents' driveway.

I was left there with myself and my daughter to care for. I hadn't had such a small responsibility in months after being George's caretaker for so long. I crumbled. I didn't have to put my own needs aside anymore because I *was* the need now. I was exhausted. I was hungry. I was weak. I was lost. I tried to function for a little while and play with my daughter on the living room floor, but I was there only in body. When George left, it felt like my spirit went with him.

Later, my dad informed me that we would be heading to the funeral home to handle the details of George's funeral. Seriously, whoever made up the rules for funerals is not cool! As soon as someone dies, there is no rest for the weary. There is always something to do or plan for, and each responsibility felt like another trauma. Dad assured me that I could sleep after we took care of the arrangements. So, I put on my big girl pants and did what I needed to do.

We arrived at the funeral home and again, another trauma. I walked in, knowing how close I was to my husband's body, and all I could think about was wanting to see him. We walked into a room full of caskets. I needed to choose a fancy box that cost and arm and a leg to lay his body in under the ground. I chose one, and on to the next thing we went. We all sat down and talked about George and his life. We wrote up his obituary that would be in the paper the next day. I am not sure why obituaries do not paint a picture of who the person actually was. Most only list the names of the survivors left behind. I was grieved by this. I wanted everyone to know how special George was and how hard he fought, not the "He lost his battle to cancer" line. That didn't reflect all the other battles he won while he was here. But once again, in my grief, I just needed to do what was required of me.

During the entire visit at the funeral home, all I could think about was wanting to see George. This was the longest I had been without him since his devastating first diagnosis, and I felt like I couldn't breathe without him. I kept looking around like I was going to see him. He was going to walk out of one of those rooms any minute, alive and healthy. I wanted to see if he had started breathing again. Was he back in one of those rooms, eyes open and breathing, unable to move and scared? Would he think I just left him and forgot about him? I kept saying that I wanted to see him. I was totally fixed on it and couldn't get it off my mind. The funeral director said something like, "She can see him if she really wants to. We have already done the embalming." I remember asking what that meant because, although I had heard that word before, I didn't really know what it entailed. The director said they had drained the blood from his body, and I began to sob loudly like I had just lost him all over again. His blood being completely gone was so final. The tricks my mind played on me about George somehow coming back to life were no longer a possibility. My dad must've talked me out of going back to see him, and we wrapped up at the funeral home and went back home.

Why?

I was a barely functioning human being and had suddenly become aware of how weak and exhausted I was. I had to get away from all the noise, so I climbed in bed to get some sleep. As I slipped under the covers, I remembered the last time I slept in that bed was next to George and began to weep again. Although his body was no longer there, the evidence of him was all around me. His clothing lying on the floor, his scent on the pillows and bedding; everywhere I looked pointed to George, but he was no longer there. I cried myself to sleep. When I woke up, I hoped it had all been a dream. When I quickly realized it was not, I went back to sleep. What was the point of being awake right now, anyway? When I did finally get up, my eyes hurt so bad because everything seemed so bright. My head throbbed. I put on my sunglasses, which helped alleviate the stress on my eyes. I remember wearing those shades around the house for several days, possibly weeks.

Happy moments only made me more upset and bitter. Laughter was my number one trigger. I didn't understand how anyone could be so filled with joy that they could let out a laugh. I hated the sun shining, people smiling, normal activities—basically anything that didn't look like grief upset me. Life went on, but I didn't understand how it could possibly continue without George in it.

McKenzie became my top priority again, and I used all my energy helping her in the aftermath of George's death. She still had a lot of questions about heaven and what would happen to her dad now. I gave her as much hope as I could, and she seemed to be doing okay until later that day. She walked out the door and let out the most gut-wrenching wail I have ever heard. I will never forget that moment for as long as I live. To see your baby suffering in such a way and not being able to do anything about it was devastating. She sobbed on the deck for a while and yelled out, "Why?" When something so traumatic like this occurs, I don't think anyone in that moment can answer why. I remember answering her whys with, "We may never know why your dad died, but we can ask God someday when we get to heaven." It was hard for me to keep it together for her when I was falling apart right beside her.

Chapter 11
The Funeral

We made it to the dreaded day of the funeral. While I never wanted this day to come, I was so looking forward to seeing George again. I headed straight to George's body the moment we entered the church. I knew he wasn't there anymore—kind of—but the lines were pretty blurred, and I am sure I started to lose it a little. His body was all I had left of him, and I wanted to take advantage of every moment I had left before it was buried and gone forever. As they opened the casket and I was reunited with him, I was heartbroken and ecstatic, all at the same time. Some people might think it is weird to kiss and hug on a corpse, and before this happened to me, I would have agreed, but this is how I grieved, and it was just going to have to be okay. I had a chair beside the casket, and people came up to pay their respects and express their sympathy to me. In the background, a few different songs played in the funeral home. One was a song George had recorded a long time ago, Celine Dion's "Have You Ever Been in Love." He loved to sing. Hearing George's amazing voice was so surreal. Every time this love song played and I heard him sing, I wept a little bit harder. It was like he was singing the words directly to me.

Our time together was so short. We both thought we had found our forever in one another, and then it ended so quickly. Another song that played—"Cinderella" by Steven Curtis Chapman—made me sob hard. George had cried his eyes out when he heard this song in the car on the way to the hospital one day. That little princess McKenzie was his world, and he did not want her to be gone once that clock struck midnight. If you listen to that song, get your tissues ready. I couldn't bear the thought of McKenzie not having a dad again. It wasn't fair, and there was nothing I could do about it.

The visitation part of the day was nearing an end, and church service for George began. I wish I could remember everything about that day and all the beautiful things and prayers that were said about him, but I just can't. I do, however, remember crying a lot and that it was a lovely service. George was truly honored that day, and that is all I could ask for. The dreaded moment of saying a final goodbye was upon us. The casket was going to close soon, and that would officially be the last time here on earth that I would ever lay my eyes on him. I couldn't even bear the anticipation of that moment. I wasn't ready, but the time was here, and it had to be done. I hugged and kissed him and didn't want to let go. I cried and yelled out, "No!" in deep, gut-wrenching heartache. You can never prepare yourself for these kinds of moments.

After the church service, we followed the hearse in the funeral procession to the cemetery. It was time to lay George's body to rest and say our final goodbyes. I was barely functioning when we arrived. I struggled to do simple things, like walk down to the burial plot; I was totally emotionally spent. I couldn't take much more. Somehow, I found enough strength to say goodbye to the closed casket once more as the burial service came to an end. As we got in our car to head back home, I had to have one final look. They lowered the casket in the ground at 4:19, and at 4:21, we pulled away. I mention those times for a reason. Do you ever look at a clock and always notice a particular time? It's almost like God is putting His finger on it, but you don't know why. Well, I have done that with three different times in my life. The times that I tend to notice are 9:11, 4:19, and 4:21. I have noticed these times for years, specifically 9:11. I noticed this time before George and I had ever even met. George passed away on 9/11, his body was lowered into the ground at 4:19, and we pulled away from the cemetery at 4:21. I don't know if this is a coincidence, or even if this is why God wanted me to notice these times, but I mention them because I have always believed these times came with warning.

We arrived home, and I no longer needed to be "strong." I took care of my duties as George's wife, and it was time to focus on myself and my daughter and begin to grieve. I put my sunglasses on and kept them on for quite some time. The light was too bright, and it hurt my eyes. Time slowed down. Hours and days seemed to pass by with little effort from me. Simply existing on this planet was all I could contribute to the world at this time.

Another Goodbye

Waking up every morning seemed pointless and devastating. Every day, I was reminded that this nightmare was my reality, and that daily reminder was too much to bear. Not long after, my sense of time went out the window. Then, we got a phone call from a coroner. They called asking to speak to my daughter directly. Thankfully, my eight-year-old daughter was at school, and I was able to take the call. I was alarmed by the message that followed. The coroner asked for McKenzie because she was listed as next of kin. I let him know I was her mother, and he delivered the news that Tim, McKenzie's birth father, had passed away overnight in his vehicle. I was shocked. McKenzie had not seen Tim since she was a baby, but now, any hopes of a restored relationship for them was gone. I made the difficult decision at that moment to not tell McKenzie and would share that information down the road when the time was right. This was just too much heartache for an eight-year-old to take in such a short amount of time. She had already endured so much trauma. I called a few of Tim's friends and family to share the news. Since we had been informed first, we needed to pass on the information from there. It was nice to reminisce about Tim for a little while. While it sort of took my mind off my current grief, I began to grieve for two people that day. A funny thing happens when someone passes away. You don't talk about the bad but instead start to remember the good about that person. It was nice, because I hadn't seen Tim in a good light for years. Tim had a hard life and passed away alone. I felt deep empathy and compassion for him. I wished life had been different for him. Although I could not change his choices, I was saddened that his life ended in that way. That day was like my funeral for him. We weren't going to attend his funeral to protect my daughter, so I said goodbye to Tim that day.

Grieving the days to follow was difficult, and I needed my own space to do so. I was so blessed to have a place to stay where my parents could help in the care of my daughter, but I also missed having a place I could call home. I was too weak and emotionally destroyed to meet any expectations that staying with someone else would require. I needed my own space to properly care for myself and my child, my way. I have always been creative and a bit messy, so my space has never been perfect, and I am okay with that. My parents, however, are perfectionists in their home, which I greatly admire, but I could not keep up with the demands necessary of maintaining a perfect space. I was operating nowhere near a hundred percent right now; I was at ten percent, tops, and I directed every ounce of that energy toward caring for Kenzie and myself the best I could. That was the only thing I could sort of manage. I soon learned that I was eligible for benefits due to the death of my spouse, and I applied. God made sure I had just enough money to afford a place for us, food, and necessary bills. I was completely broke after bills were paid at the beginning of the month, but we had what we needed, and that's all that mattered.

From Stilettos to Grace

Chapter 12
Will I Ever Be Okay Again?

Starting life over in a new space was difficult but necessary for us to properly grieve. So, we moved in. We took some items from our old condo, which gave us just what we needed to get started. Our new home wasn't perfect, but it was perfect for us, and somehow life started to feel a little more normal. Grieving, however, didn't become easier. In fact, it got harder. I didn't have any distractions to take my mind off it now. When Kenzie was at school all day, it was just me and my thoughts and, boy, was that scary…and dangerous! I teetered on the edge of insanity constantly. Driving Kenzie to and from school was my only break from the pit of hell I was in. The emotions I felt as I grieved took me as close to losing my mind as I have ever been. I was in my twenties and had now lost two husbands to death. I felt like I was cursed. I was actually scared to let anyone get too close to me because I thought maybe they would die, too. But, if I am being honest, not many people *could* get close to me. People struggled to relate to what I was going through. They didn't know what to say, how to say it, or how to comfort me, so most checked out because it was too much. I understand it now, but it was agonizing then.

I needed people more than ever, but in a lot of ways, I am immensely thankful for the time I had to lean on the Lord. During my grieving process, my faith and need for Him grew so much stronger. He became my best friend, my dad, and my husband. He had to take the wheel in my life because I couldn't. I could barely lift my head, let alone be the driver in my life. These moments reminded me of a beautiful poem called "Footprints in the Sand."[1] What resonates with me is the part of the poem where the author is saddened to see only one set of footprints in the sand, expecting to see God's also, before God reveals that those were His footprints and that He was carrying the author through a difficult time.

Looking back, I could almost feel God carrying me. I could hardly function on my own, nor could I have gotten through this time and come out on the other side without Him.

Most days went like this: I forced myself out of bed to get Kenzie ready for school and fed, and maybe I'd muster enough strength to brush my hair. After we put on our shoes and coats, we headed out the door and I drove her to school. I used this time to engage with her as much as possible. I wanted to make life as good as possible for this kid. I wanted to give her the world, but I was exhausted, deep in grief, and felt like the life had been sucked out of me. I did my best though. After arriving at Kenzie's school, I waited in the drop-off line to let her out and headed home, dragging myself back to the couch. I set my alarm clock so I wouldn't oversleep when it was time to pick her up. I spent most of

---

1 this poem has been attributed to several poets including Margaret Fishback Powers

the day sleeping because I often didn't sleep at night. This is when I got my real, good sleep. I was usually really groggy when I woke up, but I was usually the first one waiting at pick-up, so I tried not to doze off in the line while I waited. Kenzie would get in the car, and I tried to muster up any bit of joy I could find to greet her before we returned home. On the drive home, I'd ask how her day was. To be honest, I was a walking zombie. I was there but felt so out of it all the time. It was like my brain wasn't "on" most days and I was sleepwalking. It was almost like being intoxicated, in some ways, and I am sure many people thought I was. However, I had to endure this pain very much sober.

After we got home, I'd figure out something to feed her for dinner. Then, she would play for a while, get her bath, go to sleep, and we would do it all again the next day. She was a real champ during this time, going with the flow and still functioning after the loss of her dad. I, on the other hand, was barely existing. It was the best I could do.

Church

We started going to church again, and it was nice to have that as a constant in our lives. I had only just started getting plugged into church before George got sick. Once he got sick, our church visits stopped. My dear friend Charlotte recommended a grief counseling program through church, and that was extremely helpful for me. I also found a grief counseling program for kids and their families through hospice, and the program showed her she was not alone. The kids she met were in similar situations and grieving the loss of a loved one. They did age-appropriate activities like writing letters to lost loved ones, drawing pictures, and sharing about their loved one to keep their memory alive, and these activities helped her release some grief and heal. I was so thankful she had a space where she could grieve in a way that made sense to her and know that she was not alone.

These outings were a big deal for me. It took every bit of energy I had to prepare for them. Just getting dressed and trying to look presentable was a lot for me. We found some support through a cousin of mine. She had also lost her husband and her kids had lost their dad. It was good to know we weren't going through this alone, but it was sad knowing others were going through this kind of hell, too.

Days and weeks and months slipped by, and we arrived at our first holiday without George. I now understand why holidays are so hard after you lose someone. I felt so alone. As other couples gathered around the table with their respective families, it was just Kenzie and me again. I was confronted by the harsh reality that we were back at square one when it came to having our picture of what a family should look like. Thanksgiving was hard but paled in comparison to Christmas. There is so much joy and expectation around Christmas. I had to grapple with the fact that financially, Christmas was going to look a lot different for my kid that first year. I just didn't have much extra to spend. I received some assistance through a non-profit, which was amazing, and I bought her some things from the dollar store as well. It wasn't much, but I was grateful that she was going to have some gifts that year. The biggest change that stood out to me was the effect Christmas music had on me. One day while I was shopping for McKenzie, I heard all the Christmas music playing in the background. Suddenly, grief overwhelmed me, and I left the store in tears. "I'll Be Home for Christmas" began to play, and I just fell apart as the words played over the loudspeaker in the store. Those words weren't true. George was not going to be home for Christmas, no matter how badly I wanted him to be. He wanted desperately to make it to Christmas, but that didn't happen. I began to hate everything about Christmas that year and, honestly, would have loved to skip the holiday all together, and if it hadn't been for my daughter, I am sure I would have. But that kid had been through so much, and she deserved to have a normal Christmas, so I tried to give that to her.

Thankfully, the holidays passed and I rang in the new year alone and in tears. I said goodbye to the worst year of my life. The year 2008 was a living nightmare from start to finish, from George's leukemia diagnosis in January to celebrating Christmas without him. That New Year's Eve, I turned the page on the pain and welcomed a New Year, but the New Year came and my grief still remained.

The Language of Grief

That year of grief was hard. I don't think I can fully explain grief to someone who hasn't experienced it firsthand, although I wouldn't wish this hell on my worst enemy. Most nights, I couldn't sleep at all. I was alone and scared. During the day, I had to keep it somewhat together as a mom, but at night as McKenzie slept, I was losing it. My mind played tricks on me. I called out his name at every noise I heard. I thought, maybe, he was sending me a sign or something. But sometimes, hearing noises terrified me; I thought someone was going to hurt me or my daughter and I didn't know what to do. I have never been so close to insanity in my life. I woke up hopeless, I went to sleep hopeless. I had nothing to look forward to and it felt like all my dreams had died the day George died. I cried out to God, begging Him to send George back, give him messages from me, or give him a hug or kiss for me. I was completely lost and broken. If I hadn't had a relationship with the Lord, I am certain I wouldn't have survived. I believe this kind of grief would be too much for anyone to bear without Him.

As time went on, though, my heartache seemed to lessen. It wasn't that I didn't terribly miss George, but the new normal of life without him started to set in. Navigating life became a little easier. I found healing in painting, and nothing was safe—I painted on anything I could get my hands on. It gave me something to do and gave my life purpose. I painted tables, beds, canvases—anything in front of me.

Chapter 13
Feeling Alive Again

After a year went by, I started thinking about giving dating a chance again. I was so set on never marrying again that I had included my name on George's headstone. But as time passed, my heart began to soften to the idea and the dream of having a family with a mom and dad and possibly more children tugged at my mind. Just the thought was scary. I felt I was bringing a lot of baggage to the table. Whoever had the opportunity to be in our lives was going to need to love McKenzie and accept everything that came along with us—our grief and struggles as we navigated this new life we had been plunged into. I wasn't completely sold on the idea of dating, but I thought about it. I sometimes wondered who would even want the curse we carried. I knew it wasn't true—McKenzie and I were awesome gifts and weren't cursed—but it certainly felt that way after all of the trauma we'd encountered.

I talked to a couple of guys online, but nothing really came from those conversations. It was nice, however, to have someone to talk to and let some of this stuff out. I wanted to feel somewhat normal and, honestly, I needed to know someone cared. One day, an old friend of my brother's "friended" me on Facebook. Dustin and I messaged each other for a while, and he shared that he was going through a difficult time, including a divorce. At this time, I enjoyed going to Euchre (my favorite card game) tournaments on Friday evenings and invited him along to play and to hang out with us. I had known him for a long time and was sad to hear that he was going through such a hard time. I wanted to help him if I could.

We had a great time at the tournament, and my brother and his then-girlfriend invited us out to dinner afterward to a bar/restaurant that served yummy food and had a basketball court inside the building. We shot some hoops and all of us had a really great time. We went back to my brother's house for a bit and chatted, catching up on old times. We had such a great time that we stayed up the entire night talking. I didn't really want the night to end. It was so nice to have another adult to talk to and share everything we had been going through. Things seemed so easy with him. I knew his past and he knew mine. We had even gone to each other's weddings. I had often seen him at my parents' house, and he had known McKenzie since she was a baby. There was nothing complicated in sharing our "baggage."

Feeling Alive Again

That evening, I think we both realized we had feelings for each other. I always felt safe with Dustin, and he had always been such a nice guy. I used to try on my little clubbing outfits and ask his opinion before I went out dancing, back in the day. He was one of the only friends of my brother who I had any kind of friendship with. As we talked that night, he opened up and told me what he was looking for in a woman, and I was excited when I realized I fit his description. He wanted a woman who was strong, independent, and could take care of herself. Well, I could certainly do that. I had been doing that for most of my adult life. We never did sleep that night, but we did make plans to watch a movie together at my townhouse the next evening. I was so excited to spend some more time with him. I was telling him about the movie *The Notebook* and was shocked he hadn't seen it yet. We agreed to watch it together.

I was nervous, but not. It was a strange feeling. I had known Dustin for such a long time, so I was comfortable with him, but now I felt differently about him. Suddenly, we had chemistry that neither of us was prepared for.

Our movie night had finally arrived. It was kind of awkward, initially, but it didn't take long for us to get comfortable with each other. It quickly became apparent that our relationship was more than just a friendship. I was excited, but I also questioned if I was ready for more. I let down some walls and began to open my heart to the possibility of seriously pursuing this relationship. We started seeing each other nearly every day. We were falling for each other and falling quick. It was exciting, and I felt alive again. We hadn't spent much time together, but our time was enough to know we had completely fallen in love with each other, we just hadn't said it yet. We probably said we missed each other a thousand times a day, and "I miss you" had become code words for "I love you." I was scared that I would no longer be able to hold it back and suddenly burst out, "I love you!" I really wanted to wait for him. I wanted to make sure I wasn't alone in these feelings and wasn't pushing myself onto him.

One evening as we snuggled up on the couch, he finally told me that he loved me. I felt like I had just won the lottery! I told him how much I loved him and shared that I had loved him for quite a while. It was such a beautiful, special moment, and one I never thought I would have again.

McKenzie

We spent most of our time together after McKenzie had gone to bed. When she was awake, she knew we were "friends." One day, however, I discovered that she'd caught on that we were dating. She had gotten a little journal and had written something like, "Mom loves Dustin." We now knew we hadn't been so successful in our endeavor to hide our relationship. I was so worried to tell her because I didn't want her to think I was replacing her dad. I also didn't want to put her in another painful situation. She seemed completely okay with our relationship though, and the three of us began to spend a lot more time together. I was so happy to have McKenzie's approval, and it seemed like the pieces were finally coming together. I was on cloud nine, madly in love with Dustin and actually living life again. There is something about the feeling of falling in love that can't be matched. When we weren't together, we constantly messaged each other all the sweet things, and when we were together, our chemistry was undeniable.

Some time had gone by, and my year lease on the townhouse was coming up. I needed to make some decisions. Do we stay in this space for another year or do we move into Dustin's home? He had spent practically every day with us in the townhouse since we began dating. After work, he'd rush over for the evening and leave the next morning to grab a shower at his house before going to work. His house was not being used, although he was paying the mortgage every month. But was it too soon? Lord knows I did not want to make another mistake and potentially cause my child more trauma. We discussed it with each other and our loved ones, and after running the idea past McKenzie, her excitement confirmed that moving in together was the best decision.

Fresh Start

Soon after this decision, we began the moving process. As our two worlds merged into one, we had to adjust our lives to reflect this change. Some of my belongings were from my previous marriage, and Dustin's house was still set up the way it had been during his previous marriage. So, we moved some things around and made it work. It didn't necessarily feel like home yet, but it was a safe, secure place filled with the people I loved, and for that I was thankful.

During this time, I decided to go back to school. I didn't want to waste the time I had, and I wanted a fresh start. After much reflection and research, I decided to become a cosmetologist. This seemed like a perfect fit for me as an artistic person who loves to socialize. Earning my certificate would take a year, and then I could take my state board testing and start working in the field right away. It was exciting, and I felt a sense of empowerment. I began school and loved learning everything. The curriculum was designed to teach students about services including haircuts, hair coloring, perms, hair styling, and nails. It was so exciting! In fact, I felt like I appreciated school more and took it so much more seriously than many of my peers. This really meant something to me. I had my baby at nineteen and had focused on the responsibility of taking care of her. I never had the chance to chase my dreams. Motherhood was so important to me, and I would do it all again in a heartbeat, but I wasn't going to waste this moment now to focus on myself. I embraced every minute of learning. I quickly rose to become one of the top stylists in my class. I threw my whole self into it. I loved so many of the skills I learned during my studies, but my absolute favorite service was hair styling, or "formal updos." I loved manipulating hair into a work of art. There was so much you could do to transform the hair and person. Plus, if you weren't satisfied with one hairstyle, you could undo it and begin again with a blank canvas. I participated in a few creative hair styling contests and even won a few during my time at school.

During formal dance season, I often stood at the front door of the cosmetology school, trying to get as many updo clients as I could. I loved when a client sat in my chair and completely trusted me with their hair. I made some sweet friends during this time, and it was so nice to not only work toward a goal but also feel like an adult again. For so long, it had been mostly me and my little one—which was great—but to have girlfriends who you could laugh, cry, and talk with was priceless.

My time in school finally came to an end. I was sad to leave the friends I had made but eager to kickstart my future career. I hit the books and prepared for my state board test. This exam was not for the weak. Hours of studying went into it. Honestly, I felt like we had to know more about sanitation and disinfection than a hospital. Probably not, but they were serious about it. We learned everything from nail and skin diseases to sanitation and disinfection practices, and so much more—and that was just for the written part of the test. After that, we had to demonstrate several techniques on mannequins. It was a nerve-wracking test, and I was beyond grateful to have passed it. The certificate I earned would allow me to work in a salon under the supervision of another stylist for six months, and then I would need to return to test again for a certification that allowed me to work on my own. So, I began my career as a hair stylist.

Chapter 14
Another Chance at My Dreams

Everything was going great. My relationship with Dustin was good, and I had a job doing something I really loved. However, my biological clock started to tick, LOUDLY. I felt a sense of urgency to get married and start a family. When George passed away, I thought my opportunity to have more children passed away with him that day. But things were different now. That dream of having more children was alive in my heart again, and I was ready to begin, but "first comes marriage."

Dustin and I talked about it and decided that we were going to elope. We both had been married before and didn't want to make a big deal of it, so we booked a trip to Las Vegas. He sweetly asked McKenzie if he could marry her mom and then took her engagement ring shopping to pick out a ring. It was so important to us that she felt included and that her feelings were heard. She said yes, I said yes. We were all excited.

A couple weeks later, Dustin and I headed out to Vegas to make it official. Neither one of us had ever been to Las Vegas before, and while we didn't find the city particularly awesome, we knew we could get married quickly and affordably there. We found a place, and part of their service included a limousine to pick us up. From there, we would stop at the courthouse for our marriage license before going to the wedding chapel. We began getting ready for the big day. I had found a gorgeous, formal, white prom dress at a store that looked just like a wedding dress. We were ready to go and went down to the lobby to wait for the limousine. This was one of my favorite moments in Vegas.

What Happens in Vegas...

When we entered the lobby of the hotel, the first thing people saw was a bride—so appropriate for Vegas. People wanted to talk to us and take selfies with us. It was a cool time, and although we didn't have any family with us, it kind of made me feel special for our big day. Every bride wants to be gushed over on their special day, and I was no exception. The wedding service was simple and sweet, and we really enjoyed our day. We had a nice dinner that evening at the hotel to celebrate and spent the rest of the trip having fun. We did some gambling, saw a show, and did a couple touristy things together. Now, we were ready to come home and start our life together.

About a month after arriving home, I started to feel a little different and nauseous. Wouldn't you know it, whatever happens in Vegas doesn't always stay in Vegas! I was pregnant and ecstatic. To me, it really was a dream come true. It wasn't long before then that George had died and I thought my dreams of more children had died, too, but here I was, getting another chance at life. Dustin was very excited, too, and I just knew he was going to be a great dad.

That same day, I went to the hospital to meet my brother's first child, Henry, and told my family that Henry would soon have a new cousin to play with. It was such an exciting time. It seemed fitting because our first date was with my brother and his wife.

I made a special shirt for McKenzie that said "Big Sister" to announce the pregnancy to her. We were all on cloud nine! I continued to work and build my clientele until I was about to pop. Seriously, I was so big that I had a hard time highlighting my client's hair because my belly wouldn't let me get close enough to them.

God's Hand

My pregnancy was a little rough. I had major heartburn, and for the first (and hopefully last) time in my life, I got kidney stones. It was one of the most painful experiences in my life. Thank God I only had to deal with them for a few days. They were so bad I begged to be admitted to the hospital, but because I was pregnant, there was little they could do to treat me, so they sent me home. My sweet boy was due in March, and were we ever ready for his appearance! I was very uncomfortable those final weeks. The doctor decided to induce me around his due date because I was having contractions but not making much progress. This is where things went wrong—but could have gone a lot worse. I believe we may never realize the miracles the Lord performed for my sweet family that day.

Overnight, they began the medicine that would (hopefully) help me progress. At first, the contractions seemed easy, and I felt confident I could manage the pain without drugs. Boy, was I wrong! The doctor came in that morning and said I hadn't made any progress at all and she was going to break my water. The moment after she did that, all hell broke loose. I felt the most excruciating pain I had ever felt in my life. I think being shot would have been less painful. I knew I wouldn't be able to handle this for long. Something felt wrong. Labor pains hurt with McKenzie, but nothing like this. I asked the nurse to immediately to order the epidural, and I believe she sensed something was wrong, too, because she decided to check me. When she did, she quickly felt something wrong and, in a panic, made things much worse.

The umbilical cord was coming out before the baby. This is called a prolapsed cord and statistically only happens in less than 1% of pregnancies. She knew she had made the situation worse by pulling the cord further out and had to push the cord back up immediately, I assume to release tension from the baby. In a tearful panic, she told Dustin to push the "code" button and to grab the oxygen for me. She said things were not good and I would need an emergency C-section immediately. My mom and daughter arrived at the hospital just in time to see a team of doctors flood into my room as they were pushed out of it.

The doctors tried to get the cord back in place by having me flip over onto my knees, but it wasn't working. Off we rolled down the hall in what seemed like a blur. The nurse had her arm still inside of me, holding the cord in place as much as possible as we wheeled down the hall frantically. Did I mention I hadn't gotten the epidural yet? We arrived in the surgery room, and the nurses and doctors were waiting for me with worried expressions. While they sounded panicked, they told me to remain calm. I was calm, so I looked at them and told *them* to calm down! I've had my fair share of emergencies, so I was pretty good with handling critical situations. The last thing I heard was the doctor saying, "Let me know when I can cut." That's when I became nervous. I was fully awake with no drugs in my system. I think I blurted that out to them, and the next thing I remember is waking up in recovery in a tremendous amount of pain.

As soon as I opened my eyes, I wanted to know where my baby was and if he was okay, and where Dustin was. My throat was so sore from being intubated that it hurt to talk, but I needed to know. I imagine they were quick about shoving the tube down my throat, as they needed to get baby out as quickly as possible. They brought in my husband and my baby. He was perfect! They were all shocked that he was okay and even alive. They had prepped the NICU (Neonatal Intensive Care Unit) for his arrival and let them know that a baby would be coming in, in bad condition. When they tested him, however, his results came back perfect on everything. After they made sure he was okay, they sent him in to be with me.

So Blessed!

We were so blessed that the situation had not been worse. Apparently, prolapsed cords, if not dealt with at once, can kill baby and mom quickly. The pain that followed that day was rough, and they had me on a PCA pump to receive very strong pain meds. My body had been through so much trauma, and I felt it. Family came in and met our perfect little boy, whom we named Lincoln, and they were all so happy we were both okay. His birth was nowhere close to what we had pictured would happen, but the result was worth it. I had to stay in the hospital an extra day due to the pain I was in, and little guy was dealing with some jaundice and needed a little extra care, too.

After three days, we were able to bring home the most precious baby boy, Lincoln, and begin living as a family of four. It was such a sweet time. That sweet little boy needed a lot of attention, though. He did not want anyone other than his momma. Either the trauma from his birth or stomach issues made that little guy super high maintenance. I rocked him all day long. When I was hungry, Dustin would make me a sandwich and bring it to me so I could eat while I was rocking him. If I could have nursed him around the clock, he'd have been okay. Wow, was I exhausted! I have never seen a child who needed his mom so much and was not satisfied with anyone else. I loved the way he loved me, though. He made sure to let me know how needed I was, and after wanting a baby for such a long time, that was a welcomed feeling. When I tried to jump in the bathtub for for some time to myself, my husband would have to bring little Lincoln to me because he couldn't get him to calm down.

After about six weeks, I went back to work on Saturdays to get some of my clients in, but that did not last long. That little guy of mine was not having any of it. By the time I got home, he was so worked up that it would take me an hour or more to soothe him. Even after I nursed him and he fell asleep from exhaustion, he still made the little sounds you make after a big cry. It was pitiful. I tried leaving a shirt with my milk smell on it for Dustin to comfort him, but that didn't work either, so we decided I would stay home for a little while longer.

Not long after Lincoln was born, we found out we were expecting again. We were so excited because we wanted to have another baby soon. But before we could make any announcements or even make it to the first doctor's appointment, I began cramping and bleeding a ton. I knew what it meant, and I screamed and cried. We got into the doctor right away and the news we dreaded was confirmed—I was no longer pregnant. It was heartbreaking. Although we had only known we were pregnant for a short while, we were so happy and already in love with that baby. To learn that precious gift is no longer there is devastating. We continued to try for another child, and nine months after our precious Lincoln was born, we found out we were expecting yet again. This time, my pregnancy was going well, and we were able to tell family the big news. We told McKenzie first at her birthday party. We dressed Lincoln in some adorable overalls, and underneath he wore a cute little shirt that said "Big Brother." As she opened her gift from us (a matching "Big Sister" shirt), I unlatched Lincoln's overalls to reveal the big news. She was so shocked! She had been an only child for such a long time, and now she was going to be the big sister to two siblings.

Another Girl

This pregnancy went well, besides some heartburn, everything went smoothly. I really wanted to treasure this pregnancy because I thought it may be my last one, so I wanted to do all the fun things like a gender reveal party. When it came time to find out the gender of our baby, we ordered a cake that would be either pink or blue on the inside to reveal what we were having. We had a little get together at a local restaurant and invited close family members to attend. We gave McKenzie the honor of cutting the cake and had each person wear a color to represent what they thought we were going to have. McKenzie cut the cake, and before even pulling a slice out, she started jumping up and down with joy as tears welled up in her eyes. She already had a little brother, and our newest addition was going to be a GIRL. We were thrilled! I wanted to try having a vaginal birth again, but unless I delivered before the actual scheduled due date, I would likely have another Cesarean.

We scheduled the delivery for August 28, and it looked a lot different than my delivery with Lincoln. No emergency situation, and for the most part, everything went perfectly. Dustin was able to be in the room to witness the birth, and other than a little discomfort, I felt okay too. The doctor pulled out our beautiful baby girl and commented on how pretty she was. We were overwhelmed with joy and pride. It was such a special moment, and the births of each of my children are among the best moments of my life.

The family all came into the recovery room to meet our sweet girl, and the most special meeting was when

McKenzie and Lincoln met their little sister. Lincoln was a busy little guy at this time. He was eighteen months old and got into everything. He didn't like to sit still for even a minute. He was very curious about this little baby in mommy's arms though and wasn't sure that he wanted to share me at first. Charity, our newest baby girl, came out a little caretaker. When her brother fussed and threw tantrums, she stopped crying and let me tend to her brother's needs first. We were thrilled to take this precious little girl home, and now we were officially a family of five. My stay-at-home mom job became a little more challenging when Dustin left for work. I was officially outnumbered and exhausted. I now had a newborn, a toddler, *and* a teenager. Lord, help me! It was so worth it, though. Charity was a really good baby, and she was definitely more independent than her big brother was. I tried to rock her to sleep sometimes, but she wouldn't be still until I put her down. Then, she would put herself to sleep. This was so hard for me to accept because one of my all-time favorite things to do was hold a baby, but Charity liked to be put down more often than McKenzie or Lincoln ever did.

From Stilettos to Grace

Chapter 15
Shadows of the Past

I began to experience emotional changes as I settled into having three children. I couldn't seem to put my finger on what the problem was. I just began to feel anxious about everything. Life was good and things were fine with the family, but I started to think about the worst-case scenario in every situation. I constantly checked my surroundings and didn't trust anyone. At first, I thought I was just using wisdom. If my past had taught me anything, it was to not trust anyone because there were a lot of bad people out there. I looked at the world through the lens of a former stripper and victim of sexual abuse. Obviously, this was not a healthy way to navigate life, but this was my experience. Maybe having babies triggered this inside me. Maybe it was Kenzie being a teenager that triggered me. I couldn't figure out why memories from the past were coming up now. It wasn't unusual for my past to come up from time to time, but I usually found a way to push it back down and move on with my life. But this time, for some reason, I could not stuff it all down anymore. I was always on the verge of what felt like a panic attack. I felt so guilty. I should have been enjoying every moment of having these babies, but most of the time, I was so overwhelmed that I couldn't focus on the positives. I felt like I was drowning.

Life, however, continued. Shortly after Charity's first birthday, along came another surprise. It's difficult to put into words just how surprised we were. We found we were expecting again. We were shocked. My husband had undergone a vasectomy procedure just a few months prior, so we thought we weren't going to be having more children. When we made that decision, we were grieved by the thought of never having any more children. But God had a different plan in mind, and we were so grateful He did.

We announced the news to my family on Thanksgiving that year. Everyone was excited, as well as shocked, because they knew about Dustin's procedure. By the time sweet, miraculous Jasmine was born, I had a fourteen-year-old daughter, a three-year-old son, a twenty-two-month-old daughter, and a newborn. It was such an exciting time, but to say we were exhausted was an understatement. She was such a sweet baby, and we all fell in love with her. I had started taking baby photos before this, and when Lincoln was a baby, I had really made a name for myself as a photographer. By the time Jasmine showed up, I was *really* good at newborn photography. I enjoyed dressing her up and having her model all the different sets and props I had. That newborn stage was my favorite with all my kids. It was such a special bonding time with each of them. During that early little stage, they were so dependent on me, and part of me needed them as much as they needed me. I didn't mind the sleepless nights most of the time because I knew how fast that stage would be over. Jasmine was such a beautiful addition to our family, and I am so thankful to the Lord for the miracle of her life.

Woman Camp

Remnants of my abusive past began to surface even stronger after Jasmine was born. Someone could touch me, and I my whole body would clinch up tightly. I didn't know what to do about it, but I knew something was very wrong with me. Once in a while I did a Bible study, which seemed to help a little. I promised myself and the group that I was going to call a counselor and get the help I needed, but I never could follow through. Trauma has a way of putting so much shame on you that if you share any darkness, you think everyone around you will hate you or think you are the worst person in the world.

We had started attending a new church not long after Jasmine's birth, and we were really enjoying it. I even began to feel a little better. This was big for us. I'd had a relationship with Jesus for a while now, but since Dustin and I got together, I stopped going to church. I talked to God a lot, but there is something about being in church that helps put your focus back where it should be. In in some ways, this was my coming back to Christ moment. I began to have a sense of hope in my life more regularly and even began to believe He could heal me from the trauma I suffered, too.

One of the services the church offered was Woman Camp. My husband had gone to Man Camp before and loved it, so he encouraged me to go. As a girly-girl, camping out in the wilderness did not seem like my idea of fun. They advertised the camp at every service, and soon, women began sharing their stories about how God healed them at camp and their lives were forever changed. I decided I had to try it; I had nothing to lose. I had so much shame and darkness inside of me I was slowly drowning and wanted so desperately to be whole again. Remember when I mentioned healing in the first chapter? Well, this is where my healing journey began.

Going to this camp would be the first time I ever left my kids overnight, but if I came back healed, it would be worth it. I wanted to make the most of my time at the camp, as the experience would be less than twenty four hours long. After we hiked in, we had our first talk of the event, which really resonated with me. I will never forget the speaker telling us to go deep, fast. She encouraged us to make the most of our time and hold nothing back. After the talk, we did an exercise that involved putting a veil on our heads and then burning it at the campfire. The veils represented the masks we wore to hide our true selves. Most people burnt their veils quickly, but I wanted to take my time. I did not want to take this lightly. I had been wearing a mask for so long that no one really knew me. I was tired, and I could no longer navigate my healing journey alone. When I approached the prayer tent and asked my prayer partners to help me burn my veil, I let it all out, right then and there. I thought this was going to be the moment I was forever healed, and while that's not quite what happened, that day marked the start of something beautiful. I didn't hold back as I revealed the skeletons in my closet to my group. I told them about the sexual abuse, the rape, the stripper thing, the pain over the death of my husband—everything! All that darkness came pouring out. I had finally shared it and, somehow, that act began the healing within me. I learned I could share all the bad stuff and would be met with love. My group still accepted me, and some even became my friends after camp. I tasted a freedom unlike any other, and I wanted more. I couldn't go backward—only forward. I came home, and although I knew there was much more healing to come, I knew that it had begun. The sleepless nights continued and at times, my skin crawled when someone touched me.

One Night

One night, in another one of my sleepless fits, I began to research the support groups advertised on my church's website. We always talked about joining a group at church, and I think this was God's way of reminding me to look into it. I discovered a group called CST, which stands for Childhood Sexual Trauma. I immediately signed up. I was scared to death, but I knew if I didn't sign up right then, I never would. Walking into that class was one of the scariest things I ever did. It felt like my secret was no longer a secret and the world knew now. I watched as others entered the church, and I was heartbroken that so many people were hurt the way I was. It was so surreal, knowing I was not alone on this journey anymore, that others around me in this class would understand what I was going through. Still, I was so scared I didn't dare utter a word to anyone. Every week, the class featured professionals who worked with sexual abuse survivors, and when they discussed the symptoms and side effects of abuse, it was like they were reading my mail. For once in my life, I felt known, and I was just happy to hear I wasn't crazy. I felt validated knowing my triggers were normal side effects of trauma. It was still so painful though. I was not only the victim of this horrible abuse, but now I had to deal with all the brokenness that came from it. The task felt big and overwhelming, like an impossible mountain to climb. I looked around the room and saw victims—some twice my age—and felt defeated. I couldn't believe that some people had spent their whole lives healing from abuse, and I wondered if I would be subjected to that fate as well. It felt like a death sentence sometimes, like I was imprisoned by this abuse for the rest of my life.

It wasn't all doom and gloom though. The class also shared ways to heal from the abuse and provided the tools we needed to deal with triggers when they arose. They gave us contact information for different counselors in the area, and they encouraged us to explore therapy, including options I had never even heard of before. I was hopeful and passionate about my journey of healing from this brokenness. I would not be a victim forever but an overcomer and a survivor. The group was amazing, but I knew afterward that my healing journey had just begun. I still had a lot of work to do. I felt God with me in every step I took toward healing.

After the CST class, I found a local counselor who accepted my insurance, and after some background from me, we would begin doing a therapy together called EMDR. EMDR stands for Eye Movement Desensitization and Reprocessing, which can be done by using light, sound, and even tapping. In my non-technical explanation of my EMDR experience, the therapist guided me back into the trauma during the session, which allowed me to relive it and deal with it in a healthier way. After this exercise, the brain can store the experience away so I would no longer be living out of that trauma.

EMDR therapy was quite successful for me, and after eight weeks, my counselor agreed that I no longer needed to see her. I was so relieved, in more ways than one. Shame and guilt no longer had a hold on me. Fears lessened in my life, and even being touched no longer sent me climbing the walls. Unfortunately, the triggers returned sometime later, and I felt so defeated because I was technically doing all the right things. I was getting help, working hard, and finding forgiveness for the abusers in my life, but my body just wouldn't forget the pain. Almost every touch caused my body to relive the trauma of the abuse, and it was hardly bearable. A counselor at the CST group explained it perfectly when she said living with trauma was like putting your hand on a hot stove and trying to keep it there. I didn't want to feel this way every time my husband or kids tried to hug or touch me. I hated it! It was not only hurting me but everyone around me. I felt especially bad for my husband. He was so supportive and understanding, but sometimes the rejection affected him, and I felt helpless because I couldn't fix it. I tried and tried, but I just couldn't get that PTSD to leave.

At this point, I had gone as far as I could on my own. My healing had to come from a miracle from God. I started attending every prayer and worship night offered by my church or another local ministry. I was an open wound, and these prayer experiences became my Band-Aid to get me through to the next one. I asked for prayer to heal my PTSD every chance I got. I didn't care how I looked anymore; I was desperate. I must have looked like an addict looking for my next fix, and in some ways, I felt like that. These prayer Band-Aids kept me functioning as a human being. I needed to be a wife and a mom, and without these "fill up" nights, it was like running on empty.

Chapter 16
A New Beginning

I felt like I was at the end of actions I could take to help myself. I had done everything I could think of to find healing from this PTSD, but what I was doing just wasn't cutting it. I wasn't passive in my endeavors, either. I was all in. I chased the healing with everything I had. I wanted so desperately to be whole, and I had so many people counting on my wholeness, there was no turning back now. I wanted to help others who had been sexually abused as well, but my story didn't feel complete without the happy ending of wholeness. I wanted others to know complete healing was possible. I had gone as far as I could go though, and while I continued to step forward, the ultimate healing would come in God's timing. I reached out to a friend I had met through CST. I knew she had been abused and thought maybe she could help me. She invited me over, and I sat with her and her husband and shared a bit more of my story. They listened, encouraged, and prayed for me. They also told me about a ministry in Georgia they thought would help my situation. They were so empathetic and wanted my healing so badly that they offered to sponsor me to go.

Driving Down to Georgia

No one had ever taken a chance on me like that before, and after talking to my husband, I decided to take them up on their offer and go. Inside, I knew this ministry was the key to my healing, but I was a bit skeptical, too. How could this deliverance retreat be the answer for my healing? I made the six-hour drive down to Georgia and talked to God along the way.

"Why do I have to drive all the way to Georgia just to be healed?" I asked Him. I felt Him remind me that people in the Bible walked on foot for days just to catch a glimpse of Jesus, and here I was in an air-conditioned vehicle with snacks and all my comfort items. I stopped questioning at that point and became more expectant of my healing.

I remembered the Bible verse and story God had given me at the beginning of my healing journey: "And he said to her, 'Daughter, your faith has made you well; go in peace.'" (Luke 8:48 ESV)

If you have not read this story in the Bible, I encourage you to—it is one of my favorites. The daughter in this story had spent twelve years seeking healing from a blood-related ailment. She had gone to many doctors and professionals and still was not healed. Maybe she had found a little bit of healing along the way like I had, but her healing was not complete. In Mark 5:26 NIV, the Bible says that "she spent everything she had, yet instead of getting better she grew worse." In those days, a woman's bleeding was considered unclean, and she would have to announce her uncleanliness every time she journeyed out.

Let's just pause right there for a second. Can you imagine suffering for twelve years, doing everything humanly possible to find healing, only to still suffer? Can you imagine the shame she must have felt every time she left the house, and how much courage and faith she needed to walk out in the streets and announce that she was unclean? I imagine some days, this burden was too heavy, and I am sure that over those twelve, long years, she may have wanted to give up so many times. But something inside of this woman's spirit wouldn't let her quit. I can so relate to that! In my journey, there were many times I wanted to call it quits, but something inside me knew that God wouldn't have brought me this far just to leave me without my healing. I believe this woman knew that, too.

Back to the story. The woman heard about Jesus coming into town and thought, *If I could just touch the hem of His cloak, I will be well.* So, she journeyed out once again, full of hope, only this time her confidence in her healing had grown. She knew deep inside, just touching Jesus would change everything. And finally, just like that, she received her healing. Jesus knew her story and said, "Daughter, your faith has made you well." What do you think He meant when He emphasized her faith? Merriam-Webster's definitions of faith stood out to me: 1. Firm belief in something for which there is no proof. 2. Something that is believed especially with strong conviction.

For this woman to still have faith after twelve years is remarkable. Jesus acknowledged that, too.

The Day of Retreat

I was filled with anticipation as I arrived for the first day of the retreat. On day one, we were given a lot of information, and by the time I walked out and went to bed, my brain was fried. The second day was the day of deliverance. It was pretty uneventful. There were some more talks in the afternoon, and as we left for dinner, one of the leaders said something like, "Put your pleaser hats away for the healing night tonight and come expectant." The Holy Spirit was really highlighting to me the idea of being expectant. I skipped dinner and instead went back to my room for a relaxing bath in preparation for the healing night. I put on my shirt that said "Spirit Lead Me." I also have a "Spirit Lead Me" tattoo on my right wrist. These are lyrics from a song called "Oceans" by Hillsong. It had always spoken to me, and my tattoo would be a great reminder for any time I felt like I didn't want to be led by the Spirit.

I walked into the healing night with great anticipation and faith. I needed healing, and I was not going to leave this retreat without it.

They started with a couple rounds of general healing prayers before the leader invited us to ask for specific physical healing prayer. When I raised my hand and cried out for prayers for healing my PTSD, he said he could only pray for physical healing. Then, he said they could pray for my indigestion or for my brain healing, so I said, "Brain healing, please." But how in the world did he know I had heartburn? I had just taken a heartburn pill in my hotel room prior to coming down to the healing night. The people who requested prayer were to sit down, and others came around to pray for them. The moment I sat down, "Oceans" by Hillsong began to play, and I wept. In that moment, I knew I was finally going to be healed from PTSD. A woman named Amanda prayed for me, and she was the only alumnus who came back that evening for the healing night. She later told me later she specializes in praying for the brain. When she laid her hands on my head and began to pray, I felt electricity in my brain and knew something was being rewired. I continued to weep, but it wasn't a sad cry; tears were just pouring out of my eyes. I had never experienced that before. She walked away, and I knew I was healed.

Everything is Different

I came home from that weekend, and everything was different. I had emotions again. I felt things I hadn't felt in years. I could also be touched again without going into fight or flight mode. It took a long time, a lot of work, perseverance, and a whole lot of grace from God to get here. God gave me my miracle moment, and my life was forever changed. My experience also taught me that I can do everything physically possible to achieve something, but without Him, my effort is nothing. My abuse no longer had a hold on me, and I could freely share with others what God had done for me. You see, He wastes nothing. Even the bad stuff in our lives, He will use, if we let Him. It became very important to me to encourage others. Remember when I started my healing journey and I thought I was too far gone to be healed; that there was no way I could climb that mountain on my own? I felt like I had too many traumas, made too many mistakes, and honestly, deep down inside, wondered why God would want to heal me. I was right about one thing—I could never have climbed that mountain on my own. I needed Him with everything in me, and I leaned on Him with everything I had. He was gentle along the way in this healing journey.

You're probably waiting for me to say, "And she finally lived happily ever after." Right? Well, not quite. In some ways, life was much harder after I came home. I hadn't experienced such deep feelings in years and was almost numb. The "Novocain" had now worn off, and every offense felt like a deep stabbing. I could no longer stuff things down and carry on. The emotions I experienced stopped me in my tracks and needed to be dealt with and felt immediately. However, I was living. I was no longer a zombie, sleepwalking, just going from point A to point B. I was fully alive and fully aware; fully present and fully awake. The little moments I often ignored or missed began to mean something. Before, I needed a BIG, exciting experience just to feel anything, but now, something small like kind words or a hug left me in tears because of how precious it is to me.

Hot But Manageable Mess

I don't want you to think everything is perfect now that I finally had my miracle moment. I was healed from PTSD, not all my flaws. Life still has its challenges, and I am still learning and growing as I go. Let me be clear—I am still a hot mess. What is different now is the overwhelming fear that came with the PTSD had loosened its ugly grip on me. I can now make decisions based on what I want instead of letting fear limit what I am capable of. I am not sure fear ever completely goes away, but the freedom and healing I have received makes it no longer feel like a boulder that I can't get out from under. My story doesn't end here; is far from over, and in some ways, it almost feels like it had just begun. The traumas I endured, coupled with fear, were constantly whispering in my ears all of my limitations. With those things gone and wholeness in sight, I can now hear what God says about me. The King of the universe that abides in me is limitless, and through His limitlessness, I am, too.

I want to take a moment to encourage you. If you have ever been sexually abused or have experienced any kind of trauma in your life, stop treating just the side effects of the trauma. I don't mean to say stop listening to your doctor and stop taking any medication you may be on. As you read in my story, I experienced depression, anxiety, suicidal thoughts, eating disorders, cutting, and PTSD as *side effects* to my trauma, as well as a number of other things such as jealousy, lack of trust, control issues, and I am sure the list goes on and on. Treating the *symptoms* will not ultimately heal the root. Whatever that root looks like for you—maybe it is sexual abuse, the death of a family member, or divorce— go after that trauma and the main issue and bring God in on it. The Lord met me every single step I took toward healing. He was there in the ugly in a way no one else could be, and He will be there for you, too. Invite Him into your healing process, and He is mighty to save. I know healing right now for some of you may seem so overwhelming, but it doesn't have to be. Make a plan with God and simplify it. One step at a time is all you need to take.

One more amazing truth from Luke 8:48: "And he said to her, 'Daughter, your faith has made you well; go in peace.'" I often wondered why the woman's name was never mentioned in the text. Why didn't Jesus call her by her name instead of addressing her as daughter? To me, this feels very intentional, and so right. It allows you to insert YOUR name there. This verse is not only for me; it can be for you, too! It is your verse as well, and I encourage you to take it. Your faith in Jesus can make you well. It might not be instant, or even how you thought it would, but WOW, it is so WORTH it!

God bless you all, and thank you for reading my story. If this book has helped you in any way, tell a friend or family member who may benefit from reading it.

A Final Prayer I Pray for You…

"Lord God, I ask that You bless every single person reading this book. That they will be filled with the courage to start stepping out toward healing. Lord, that You would meet them along the way with every step they take. That You would send a community of encouragers to surround and encourage them in their healing process. And that You, God, would give them grace and mercy as they step into this new path. Lord, rain down Your love and grace on them and give them their miracle moment, too. In Jesus' mighty name. Amen

—Tiffany Brearton

Guest Speaker

Tiffany Brearton
www.fromstilettostograce.com

From Stilettos to Grace
Author and Speaker

Tiffany is a woman on a mission to help bring back hope into other people's lives and to share that nothing is impossible with God. As a woman who has walked through her own healing, she knows the road can be long and lonely at times but can help find the light in the darkness in all things. She is gifted with the ability to encourage and see the best in others. After hearing Tiffany speak, you will be encouraged to take your next step.

Topics:
- Testimony "From Stilettos to Grace"
- Hanging onto hope in all situations
- Taking your next step and He will meet you
- Being a safe person and boundaries

Great for:
- Keynote
- Church
- Services Conferences

FROM STILETTOS
TO GRACE

Book to Speak:
fromstilettostograce@gmail.com

Made in the USA
Monee, IL
23 August 2022

12304676R00085